A Christian Woman book
Children under Pressure

Pat Wynnejones' experience as a Christian teacher, a mother and a grandmother, has fed her growing concern for children of today. A member of the Parliamentary Group Video Enquiry into children's viewing and a freelance lecturer and writer, her other books include *Pictures on the Page* and *Children, Death and Bereavement*.

Christian Woman Books

Series Editor: Gail Lawther

Other titles in preparation

Children under Pressure

PAT WYNNEJONES

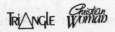

First published 1987
Triangle/SPCK
Holy Trinity Church
Marylebone Road
London NW1 4DU

British Library Cataloguing in Publication Data

Wynnejones, Pat
    Children under pressure: growing up in a
    changing world.—(Christian woman books)
    1. Children—Religious life   2. Christian life
    I. Title   II. Series
    248.8'2   BV4571.2

    ISBN 0-281-04230-6

Phototypeset by Input Typesetting Ltd, London
Printed in Great Britain by
Hazell Watson & Viney Limited
Member of the BPCC Group, Aylesbury, Bucks

*This book is dedicated to
the memory of
a happy home*

ACKNOWLEDGEMENTS

I am deeply grateful to the many parents, teachers, teenagers and children who have written or talked to me, sharing their opinions, advice and experiences. There are too many to name individually, but I remember them all and thank them. In particular I am indebted to Canon Michael Hodge, the Rev. Clive Grinham, the Rev. Gordon Jessup and Richard Wilkins for the benefit of their wisdom on many vexed questions regarding children and their upbringing; also to the Association of Christian Teachers for permission to quote from *Spectrum* and *ACT NOW*; to Valerie Riches for permission to quote from the publications of Family and Youth Concern; to the Universities and Colleges Christian Fellowship for permission to quote from *Christian Arena*; to the editorial board of Polestar for permission to draw on their material; to the Band of Hope for permission to quote from their publications; to Fontana/Open Books Original for permission to draw on their book *Child Abuse* by R. and C. H. Kempe; to Dave Parry for permission to quote from *Alternative Alternative*; to the Family Holiday Association for access to their case histories; to Grooms Homes for permission to quote from 'The Beatitudes for Friends of the Handicapped'; to Mary Reid for permission to quote from *Family* magazine; to Anne Townsend and Care Trust for helpful information; to Branse Burbridge for permission to recount his experiences published in *ISCF Viewpoint;* to *Evangel* for permission to quote Donald Carson; and to the Rev. A. R. Higton for permission to draw on his pamphlets in chapter 5. He has also kindly agreed to answer anyone who feels the need for help with regard to involvement in the occult. His address is: The Rectory, Hawkwell Parish Church, Hawkwell, Hockley, Essex SS5 4JY.

Most of all I am grateful to my own family: I have drawn upon all that I learnt from my parents and from discussion with my brother, Dr John Coulson, who shared his lifetime experience as a Student Health doctor at a London teaching hospital.

Contents

Series Editor's Foreword

Christian women are developing a new awareness of the way our faith touches every part of our lives. Women who have always lived in a Christian environment are facing up to the important issues in the world around them. Women who have found in Christ a new direction for living are seeking to sort out the problems that are hampering their spiritual growth. And many women are rediscovering the joy in using their God-given talents, in their relationships with God and with other people, and in their spiritual lives and worship. *Christian Woman* magazine has been privileged to be part of this learning process.

As a result of this deepening awareness and commitment to Christianity, many books have been published which help women to sort out what God can do for them as women, as wives, as career people, as mothers, as single women. Most of these books however have been rooted in the American culture; this *Christian Woman* series has come into being because we believe it is important that we have books that talk our own language, and are relevant to everyday life in our own culture.

Each book in this series will deal with some aspect of living as a Christian woman in today's world. I am delighted that we have been able to be part of the blossoming of God's church in this way. We hope that the books will help you as a Christian woman to overcome problems, enrich your life and your relationships, learn more of God, think through important issues, enjoy your femininity, make wise choices, and deepen your commitment to Jesus Christ.

In these books we have invited people to share what they have learned about living as Christians. Not everyone will agree with all the ideas expressed in each book, but I know that you will find every book in the series interesting and thought-provoking.

Books change people's lives – perhaps these books will change your life.

GAIL LAWTHER

Introduction

Those of us who have children and grandchildren growing up today must feel worried as we look at the world that awaits them. This book shows very clearly that we are right to be worried – it *is* worrying.

Life is going to hold problems for our children that we never knew. This makes it hard for us to prepare them. Parents may feel that for the children's sake they must follow the permissive trend and lower their standards to meet popular expectation. Insecure parents may do so for fear that their children may turn against them. This is not the answer. On the contrary, strong parents make happy children.

Our children go to school, visit friends' homes and discos, watch television, in a society where the standards of morality which were our cultural heritage have largely been abandoned. On the whole it is a disillusioned, cynical, depressed, dissatisfied society. Our job is to steer our children to the source of happiness, the place where unchanging human nature finds its image faithfully perpetuated, together with the principles which give us fulfilment. The Bible is still the spring of psychological health.

Finally, Christian parents need to get together, to share their common wisdom and find a common strength, to lift each other's burdens and to have fun. Happy parents make strong children.

A mother wrote to me:

Christian parents need all the support and encouragement they can get, as the task of a Christian involved in the bringing up of children, whether at school or at home, is an extremely hard one. It is inadequate and certainly too easy to simply hope that children will follow your example. Over and over again in the Old Testament, great men of God failed to discipline their sons, thus frustrating God's purpose.

Of course every committed Christian is aware of his or her responsibilities regarding children, but it is fatally easy in this modern world for Satan to reign in this field, so that parents are put off the idea or at least made to feel extremely guilty for being so different. As we bring up our four-year-old son, I am more and more convinced, through much thought and prayer and Bible study, that the Christian way is the right way.

She also said that the positive side of Christian family life should be emphasised – its joys and rewards – over and above the difficulties.

The first chapters of this book look at the influences which genes and background contribute to a child's make-up. The later ones at today's damaging pressures coming from outside. My aim has been to fortify our confidence that traditional Christian ideas on upbringing are not 'old-fashioned' – they are right. A happy home built on a foundation of faith is a child's best defence.

1

The Shape of the Mould

Don't let the world around squeeze you into its own mould.
St Paul

Paul's own words remind us that meeting and coping with the pressures of life is part of being human, and the learning process involved is instrumental in shaping us as we grow up. Every culture and every generation has its own sorts of pressures. Different rites of passage await the adolescent to denote that the growing years have been successfully accomplished and that he or she is now ready for the trials of maturity.

Those who have charge of the growing years need to have regard for the demands and values of their society, and these may be reflected in the rites of passage. Courage may be the prime requirement. The adolescent may have to launch himself from the top of a tree, one ankle tied to a rope of vines as he hurtles head forward towards the ground; or he may seek the red badge of courage as in Stephen Crane's book about the American Civil War. It may be the social graces that are valued: a debutante was carefully groomed for her presentation at Court; and a young man was expected to be able to drink and smoke his way through a coming of age party. Sometimes a religious ceremony – a Barmitzvah or a Confirmation – also signifies the entry into adult status.

Parents have always needed to see that the pressures on their children were not inappropriate, and until the present time they would have had the advantage of following patterns of behaviour and upbringing established by their forbears. What makes life particularly difficult for parents and youngsters in the Western world today is that they have to meet situations which produce

1

pressures quite unknown to humankind until now. It is one thing to grow up in the jungle, learning to meet the dangers of an environment which has remained unchanged for hundreds of years, and which ancestors have devised methods of coping with. It is something else to belong to a generation whose parents are bewildered by the rapidity of change.

The world is no longer even as comparatively safe and predictable as the world which followed the Second World War. Worse than the impersonal destruction of the war itself is the personal threat to the very souls of our children, in the availability of drugs, sadistic and obscene videos, and in the aggressive advance of the occult. In spite of all the dangers of the years following the Second World War – the Berlin Wall, the cold war, the conquest of Czechoslavakia – there was a background of a familiar lifestyle; standards based on Christian ethics, stable homes and the nuclear family, were still the norm. If war threatened, horrific though it might be, it was possible to have some idea of what it might be like. But over the future of our children there hangs a great big question mark. The possibility of a nuclear war has made an unprecedented addition to the 'normal' pressures on the young by adding a dimension of continuing fear and an incentive to live for the moment, without consideration of responsibilities or possible consequences of actions.

Nuclear war is not the only hazard which is new to this generation. There is far more violent crime, a high proportion of which involves the young. They cannot enjoy a country walk or a game of football with the freedom that they used to have. The threat to the personal safety of children is now so great that it was thought wise to make an alteration to the film of *The Tanglewood's Secret*. In the story, as Patricia St John wrote it, an old shepherd, Mr Tandy, approaches the little girl and engages her in conversation. This may have been acceptable years ago, but now there is the anxiety that it might encourage a child to talk to strangers – possibly with

2

tragic result. Collectively and individually it is a dangerous world.

It is also a difficult world. Past generations were able to feel purposeful because they could see a career shaping up ahead. Today's youngsters, whatever their potential, must face the possibility of landing up in the dole queue. Looking back on their schooldays they may wonder in what respect their curriculum could be said to have prepared them for a life with so much leisure.

The whole cultural scene is changing like a kaleidoscope. Within such a short time established customs have been queried and the old certainties shaken. Families, which were the backbone of the nation, are breaking up; they are under attack from various pressure groups. Women are encouraged to despise their traditional role and even to believe that they do not need their male counterparts. Men lack confidence in their heterosexual orientation. Since sexuality is such a major element in personality this confusion is all very undermining to children in their search for identity. It is a confusing world.

At one time the home provided a sanctuary where the world did not intrude. Now society can exert pressure within our own walls through the compulsive attraction of the box. The mould of permissiveness, materialism, secularism and the occult shapes the growing mind through uncontrolled viewing of television and video films. Going into schools for the Parliamentary Group Video Enquiry has given me an insight into what happens to children who have acquired a taste for their sadism and violence. They 'like the blood' they say.

Aristotle said that we must be taught our values; we learn what we ought to like and what we ought to shun. Our taste for evil and perversion or for the good and wholesome is learned by precept and example. In so many ways we are teaching our children the wrong things. Paul's advice is still psychologically sound. We should be filling their minds with that which is true and good and right and pure and lovely.

Parents themselves are not well equipped for their role because they too are bewildered. They find an increasing problem with discipline, but they don't know what has gone wrong. The current construction that is put upon loving the children, is giving way to them all along the line; giving them everything they cry for.

'We don't know what's got into her,' remarked one father, of a rebellious twelve-year-old. 'We've even given her a television of her own to have in her room. She goes up there as soon as she gets in from school, and she can watch what she likes.'

Plastic people are no substitute for the free discussion which builds real relationships and provides parents with their most powerful instrument in countering the undesirable pressures of the age.

For Christian children it is not going to be easy. Much of what we see around is strange, puzzling, scary. The Christian guidelines which were once apparent to undergird their faith and their behaviour, are not universally acknowledged today. They will stick out like sore thumbs. Yet, on the other hand, they are the ones who have something *real* to hang onto. Also, because of the lack of social constraints, it is a time of unparalleled opportunity. Their positive approach to life may well assume a special attractiveness because it is out of the ordinary.

This then is the shape of the mould. But, even before being born into it, a baby is subject to many pressures which will go to determine what sort of person he or she will become.

In My Beginning

In my beginning is my end.
T. S. Eliot

Long before our children meet with the pressures of society they will have inherited certain personality traits along with their physical attributes which will determine the way the growing child responds to circumstances.

The young mother who wheels her new baby down the street will be stopped by friendly neighbours. 'Oh, isn't he like you,' they say, or 'Just like his grandad.' We are lumbered with the beaky nose, the red hair, the delicate skin or whatever, that is passed down through our genes to make up our physical characteristics. These in turn affect personality, in addition to the inherited personality traits. For example, teasing may make the redhead more aggressive, and similarly the small boy, to overcompensate for his size. From the word go the infant carries the mark of his forbears, not only of family, but racial and national characteristics. Genetic inheritance will also affect general health, resistance to illness, and may give a predisposition to certain diseases, any of which may contribute to further pressures.

Heredity and environment

We do not know whether hereditary factors, or environment and upbringing make the major contribution to the way a child develops. Even children of the same family will differ in their intellectual ability. But most experts agree that at least some aspects of intelligence are inherited and this must make a significant contribution to the way in which the individual approaches life. However, since a child's environment also affects intelligence, a child who is not encouraged by chatter and nursery songs and stories as a baby, and who is given meagre language experience as he grows, is likely to be permanently disadvantaged. Later on, a child who is placed in a school where there is high language awareness and rich language provision, may well make better progress than a more intelligent child who is allowed to become bored, and the fulfillment of progress and praise may provide the spur to make him far more successful eventually than early predictions would have allowed. It has also been found that when children are reared in the same home situation their IQ similarity increases, even for individuals who are not blood relations. Environment makes a difference. It exerts various moulding pressures on the growing child, as will become apparent in succeeding chapters.

We also see personality traits handed down from parent to child, and such characteristics as musical or artistic ability, love of the open air, an impassioned sense of justice, warmth of heart and forgetfulness. Human nature is full of inconsistencies and illogicalities, and we don't always recognise our own shortcomings in the failings that are so noticeable to us in our children. I once complained to my brother about the way my son would so often put off till tomorrow something that could have been done today. 'Amazing!' he replied. 'Look who is his mother!'

Parents who are self-aware will know what to look out for in their children, and should have more sensitivity in dealing with it. It should be a guide in choosing schools and careers, and in protecting children from situations which would embarrass or distress them. Inherited nervousness or aggression may complicate life for the five-year-old as he starts school and begins to make new relationships. Infant teachers and school heads are aware of such problems and find it helpful when parents share with them such inherited characteristics, where relevant, together with any important events and changes which have been traumatic in the family – the death of a relative, separation or divorce, the loss of an expected baby.

Spiritual 'genes'

The influence of heredity extends beyond the physical, psychological and emotional aspects, for there is a spiritual element in this natural law. Scripture tells us that the sins of the fathers are visited upon the children, and sometimes this is only too tragically obvious, for instance where there is a drink problem or suicidal tendencies. Perhaps this seems cruel and unjust. Yet for good or ill we are predisposed to many of the traits which characterise our forbears. But Christ can release us from such a chain of cause and effect, or from the bondage of some hereditary vice.

'Now God says he will accept and aquit us – declare us "not guilty" – if we trust Jesus Christ to take away our sins . . . no matter who we are or what we have been like' (Romans 3.22).

The wonderful promise made to Abraham, 'I will bless you with incredible blessings and multiply your descendants into thousands and millions' (Genesis 22.17) still applies.

We can see how the chain of sin can be broken and replaced by a chain of blessing in the case of children from broken homes. For them a way to healing may be found in the knowledge that they have value in the sight of God; that he will be a father to the fatherless and will never desert them. A child's greatest need is for love and security. Although this may have been shattered at a human level, and the sin of the father visited upon him by depriving him of his right to two parents and a stable background, yet even such a deep hurt can be healed by the love of God channelled through the person of some caring individual. In Christ he may become a new creature, inheriting the promised blessing on his own behalf and on that of his children and his children's children.

Parental age

The age of parents when their children are born can affect their development. Parents who have waited for a long time before the appearance of the longed-for baby may incline to be over-anxious or over protective. A mother who has left a successful career in some academic field may feel insecure in her new role, and this may affect her handling of the new baby.

> I was an 'old' mum of course, at thirty, and I didn't have any experience of babies. Tom was working away from home, too. Even when I had some milk, Jamie would often keep on screaming and fight me. It was a relief to go over to bottle feeding, as he was always crying with hunger. I found the crying, particularly in the evening and night so frustrating that I even shook him hard a couple of times (which you shouldn't do!).

Such a situation may lead a mother to reject her baby, but in this case happily a minor accident brought the mother's real affection to the surface:

> I used to pray about the fact that I didn't feel any love for him. Then he scrabbled his way off his changing mat at five months and fell on his head – which made me realise we couldn't do without him!

This caring, conscientious and very frank mother told me that she found further difficulty in Jamie's determined will, a personality trait which he had inherited from her.

> He still fights me over everything and questions my authority – it just makes me lose my temper . . . At school he is very able and obviously has excellent prospects, but wastes his time and doesn't concentrate hard enough. Prayer, by me and for me, has helped me a great deal to overcome the resentment I felt towards Jamie and to love him more. My friend Susie has also had many problems with her first child Rachel. Perhaps it's something to do with older, educated mothers, who feel more guilty about everything!

Older parents are just that bit further from their children in their physical life and may feel less ready to dash about in energetic games and rompings than very young mums and dads. But they may provide a calmer atmosphere and, having had several years of adult activities, they may be prepared to forego some social engagements and spend more time reading to their children or simply talking. This can be very valuable in cementing the relationship, in giving language experience and time for reflection.

Parents who have longed and waited for their baby may find it hard not to give way to him too freely. However, they have the advantage of seeing the mistakes their friends have made and avoiding them. They have had their years of fun and can devote more time and thought to raising their offspring.

A young mother and father can be close companions to their children, but if they are very young, as many are today, they may not have reached a stage of real responsibility. Parents under the age of twenty-four are statistically a hazard for child abuse. They may be too juvenile in their emotional development to be able to be objective in their decisions about child management. Young parents may find it harder to give up an exciting party to stay with a sick child than those who have had their fill of wining and dining. On the other hand it is a great advantage to have a father young enough to take you skiing and win the fathers' race on sports day, or a mother who looks young and beautiful.

Although these generalisations are reasonable, the impact of parental age on children will itself be modified by the many variables (for example social class, intelligence, personality) which make family relationships so complex and influential.

Pre-natal and birth experience

Love begins before a child is born. There is a psychic sensitivity between the mother and the unborn child, so that her happy anticipation transmits feelings of pleasure to the baby in the womb. This sensitivity is a significant factor in the way a child's personality develops in later life. A child whose advent is regarded as a nuisance may grow up with a poor opinion of himself, whereas the child who is longed for is likely to develop emotional stability and confidence.

The child has an identity in the womb. He sucks his thumb and kicks about and is aware of the world going on outside, especially if it upsets his mother. The independent existence of children in the womb, God's purposes for them and his meticulous loving creation of each one is mentioned in several places in the Bible. For example, 'You took me safely from my mother's womb . . .' (Psalm 22.9); 'You made all the delicate, inner parts of my body, and knit them together in my mother's womb' (Psalm 139.13). Mother and father should pray together for their unborn child, and in so doing they will further the process of bonding, strengthen the ties of love.

The idea that the emotional experiences of pregnant women can affect the baby they are carrying has been held for a very long time and now there is informed support for the theory that the state of mind of the mother can affect her child. Babies in the womb are sensitive to music; they are aware of voices, and able to feel if those voices are raised in anger or are gentle and loving.

The birth itself is a supreme emotional experience for the baby, as he leaves the security and comfort he has known, to emerge into a startling new environment. The child who is delivered by Caesarean section may be spared much trauma and in consequence may have a more placid approach to life than the child of a difficult birth. A difficult birth may incline the mother to be over-protective, or, on the other hand, make her reject the child, especially if he is ailing or difficult to rear. All these factors have an influence from the child's earliest years, but they cannot be taken in isolation from other factors such as the circumstances and personalities of the parents.

Position in family

The child who arrives first in the family enjoys some advantages and is exposed to certain risks. In any event the first child is in a unique position. The Bible attaches especial importance to the firstborn. 'Dedicate to me all the first born sons' (Exodus 13.1). He will have the distinguished position of the eldest if he is followed by one or more siblings; and whether this is so, or whether he remains an only child, his beginning will claim the undivided attention of his parents. He has a flying start.

The only child misses the genial rough and tumble of brothers and sisters, but this does not mean that an only child must be a lonely child. Friends and relations, mums and toddlers clubs, and playgroups give plenty of scope for socialising. Looking back I can think of many well-adjusted 'onlies'. The only child will have to stand alone and fight his own battles, and thereby may become self-reliant, capable and resourceful, provided he is allowed to do so. However, his parents may find it hard to avoid giving him his way in most things, especially since there are no other children to be considered. The way he grows up must be partly affected by the reason for which he is an only child. It may be that a parent has died or separated and he may have to stand in for that parent in filling the empty place and sharing the decision making. It follows that an only child may be indulged on the one hand, or in other circumstances may develop mature qualities and early independence.

The first child will benefit from the fact that his parents had more time to devote to him. Their talking, reading, answering his questions and sharing books with him will give him a good language basis when he starts school. For this reason it is often the eldest child who is quicker at learning to speak, while sometimes a younger one will rely on the older to do the talking for him. Moreover, his parents are seeing for the first time the miracle of a child learning to walk, learning to talk, exploring his environ-

11

ment, growing and developing. They record his progress meticulously, they watch anxiously for any sign of unhappiness or illness. His parents' unstinted admiration and loving concern are very encouraging to the child, and major incentives to growth. When subsequent children arrive, the parents have seen it all before, and can view each day's achievements with more equanimity. They will have acquired some experience of minor ailments and will therefore communicate less anxiety. They will have learned to discriminate between a tired, hungry or angry cry, between fear and attention-seeking, and will not tear up the stairs fearing the worst every time there is a squeak from the nursery.

It may be difficult for the eldest child not to feel jealous when the next baby appears to usurp some of the attention that he has enjoyed all to himself until then. Unless this is resolved in the early years it may produce tension in the second child; if a third arrives the second child's position may not be a happy one, somewhere between the prestigious eldest and the new attraction. Sensitive parents will be watching for the responses of their children to changing family relationships and for ways of encouraging each child to build a satisfying self-image.

A child who has been involved from the start in helping to get the pram, cot and toys ready, anticipates with his mother and father the arrival of the new person in the family. Realistic preparations and relevant talk will avoid disappointment when the new brother or sister is not born old enough to be an instant playmate, or is not the longed for puppy!

Sex also modifies the effect of the position in the family. The boy who is number five after four girls will have a different reception from the boy who is the fifth of the male sex in the family. He will doubtless grow up with a different opinion of himself and his standing among his family and friends which will probably carry over into his adult relationships outside the home. Moreover the arrival of a member of the opposite sex is less likely to arouse jealousy in the previous sibling. Peter, a second son by four years, formed an unusually close bond with his new baby sister. At three years old he might have suffered emotionally when his mother's physical condition meant a six-week spell in hospital for the third birth. But, typical of the second child in his accepting nature, he spent the weeks of waiting for his mother's return in looking forward to 'his' baby. Since she arrived, with no trace of jealousy, it has been his joy to help look after her, ('May I dry her toes?'), entertain, fetch and carry for her.

The first child may be expected to take responsibility for the younger ones, or may take on that role instinctively. Jonathan took this very seriously. He fed his little brother with a bottle, then a spoon, protected him from 'rough' friends and even dreamed that his parents had gone and he had to take care of Peter all by himself. But this real devotion did not prevent some jealous twinges; nor the usual teasings and quarrellings between brothers.

Again, the eldest is often expected to set a good example, especially at the table or in company. 'Look how well Jonathan has eaten up his dinner,' I have found myself saying to a reluctant eater. And yet such comparisons may not be the most positive way of encouraging good relationships. It needs a nice balance to give the older child a reasonable pride and satisfaction in sharing the care of younger siblings, without putting too much responsibility on young shoulders. Often though, the first child takes the initiative and so naturally becomes the leader. The second child may then be able to take life more easily, feeling secure in the protection of an older brother who will take his part in quarrels and show him the ropes at school.

The second child usually has to wear the hand-me-downs, and many of the toys he finds temptingly about the house belong to his elder brother – or sister. This can be a cause of anxiety about what he can claim for his own. 'Mines,' he will say, possessively clutching at something that belongs to somebody else. Peter went through a stage when he would not wear clothes unless he was assured that they had actually been bought for him and had not belonged to his brother.

A second child, as each subsequent addition to the family, needs to be given an equal quality of attention, and encouraged to develop in his own way, not to remain in the shadow of the elder. You have to think yourself into the position of each. It can be hard on the eldest always to have to be the good example, but it can also be hard on the younger to have so often to give way. At the same time a younger child is not generally the focus of attention and life can be more relaxed. He has the benefit of what my grandmother called 'a little healthy neglect', and for that reason may acquire an equable and placid temperament. He has the benefit of the older child's experience, who has had to put the toe in first. By the time a third child arrives all the clothes are worn out, so he starts afresh with new; this may bear hard on the second child who sees the newcomer having the nice new things which he missed!

The third-born is often characterised by diffidence, especially if of the same sex as the previous two. Mother and father are unlikely to be either as anxious or as excited as they were with the other two, and the older children have already established a working relationship with each other. The third then may find himself taking on the role of an onlooker, and may seek companionship beyond the family circle. Moses, a thirdborn, certainly exhibited this diffidence in his reluctance to take on a leadership role in approaching Pharoah as God's spokesman on behalf of his people: 'O Lord, I'm just not a good speaker . . . Lord please! Send someone else!' (Exodus 4.10, 13, *The Living Bible*).

The variables and their repercussions arising from birth and sex increase with each new baby. All these possibilities need tact and insight. Difficult situations can sometimes be helped by goodnight prayers, when love and forgiveness are expressed, and a blessing sought for all.

Each child is different and each has different needs – but they also have needs in common and the greatest of these is the security that flows from being loved. We need to ask God for the wisdom to cope with this very important aspect of bringing up children. Besides arranging the blueprint of the genes, and nurturing the baby in the womb, God has also planned the birth order of our children. So, put into his hands, these may prove blessings; stabilising influences as each child encounters the pressures of growing up.

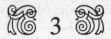

Young Olive Trees

> Look at all those children! There they sit around the dinner table as vigorous and healthy as young olive trees.
> *King David*

As parents we have to accept the fact that we are inevitably going to be the greatest influence on the development of our child's character and personality. Greater than schooling? Greater than that of friends? Even greater than all the pressures of the media? *Yes, you will be the paramount influence on the life of your child –* a challenging thought! But it also carries a measure of reassurance, together with the consciousness that that influence must be framed to produce strength of character rather than rebellion.

Your achievement will be measured in terms of your teenager's ability to discriminate among all the various influences he will meet as you launch him into the world at adolescence, and to withstand those which would be harmful. Will the Christian influence of home then provide an anchor?

How to make an anchor

The influence of parents operates through:
1 The attitudes they transmit and the care they bestow
2 Their effectiveness as models
3 The material needs, the early language experience and the learning environment they provide
4 The spiritual climate of the home

'Give me the child for the first seven years and he is mine for life' is a saying that has been attributed to the Jesuits. They perceived the marvellous potential and unique opportunity of those childhood openings, which are the

God-given prerogative of parents. Parents are closest to children during the formative years and it is usually parents who transmit to them the basic ideas and customs, values and beliefs of their society. It is in the give and take of family life that the most important aspects of personality take shape.

Getting along together

Right from the start, mum and dad and the children have to learn to get along together if the home is to be the sort of happy place which is the perfect medium to produce a happy disposition. It is a process which works both ways. Parents influence children and children influence their parents. A baby who is very slow in feeding will make his mother anxious and her anxiety will rub off on him. As a result his digestion will suffer and he will become upset and tearful. His sleep will be disturbed, and the mother will also lose her rest. Lasting patterns of behaviour can be produced in this way.

When children start school a similar tit-for-tat syndrome may arise over homework. An over-anxious parent makes a child nervous. He cannot think and becomes quite stupid, for panic makes the brain cease to function. This infuriates the tired parent who knows very well that his child is not as stupid as he seems, and suspects him of trying to get out of it. It is time to call a halt. I am very grateful both for a father who loved to help me, and for a mother who used to shut my books up and say 'That's enough for tonight,' when she saw us getting frayed.

In all such situations, a parent who can take a fairly relaxed attitude is likely to help a child to feel confident; a critical and exacting one to undermine the child and make him unsure of himself. Research has shown that 'Schoolboys whose parents' attitudes were rated "favourable" turned out well, and of those whose parents' attitudes were rated "unfavourable" almost all were neurotic, psychotic or chronically delinquent' (R. S. Illingworth in *The Normal School Child*).

17

Blowing your top

In family relationships it is the degree of understanding which exists between the members that makes quarrels and upsets into trivial ups and downs or alternatively into major rows. Some families have frequent quarrels and rows which flare up and die down as quickly. Everyone recognises this, forgives and forgets and knows that it doesn't really matter.

There are other homes where feelings are more inhibited, but if some disagreement does arise an air of resentment can cloud the atmosphere for days. This sort of oppressive silence is more likely to affect the child's approach to life and ability to make easy relationships outside the home. And this kind of emotional tension may be a particular hazard in Christian families where it is felt to be wrong to show anger and no one dares to let off steam.

However much you love a child there are times when it is almost impossible to show that love because he is being so difficult. On the other hand the child cannot bring himself to be obedient or friendly while his parents seem harsh or withdrawn. A stalemate can occur. In just such a situation we should try to remember that God did not wait until we were all reformed characters before he sent his Son. It was while we were yet sinners that Christ died for us. It is up to the parents to make the first move to reconciliation, rather than to insist on an apology which the child is, at that moment, incapable of making. There are times, too, when parents should be saying sorry, maybe to each other or maybe to the children. It may be hard, but it's good to show them that we're human after all. A golden rule is never to let quarrels stew away through the night. Everything should be sorted out before those goodnight prayers are finished.

We need to work at creating happy relationships because the atmosphere of the home is so important. Then, in times of stress, other pressures coming from outside will be less likely to act as a catalyst to trigger off a damaging row.

Hoping all things

We need to think ahead during the childhood years and prepare ourselves as well as our children for their adolescence. Our idea of what this may entail is important, for children respond so readily to what they think you expect of them and they are very sensitive to the 'vibes' we give off. Expect disaster and you will probably get it. Let your children see that you believe in them and trust them, and they will not let you down. A Christian home is no guarantee against adolescent problems, but where mutual trust has been the keynote of the childhood years, children as they mature will naturally align themselves with the values of the home and see the secular world with its deluding pressures as the opposition – rather than their parents.

Unfortunately, we have been conditioned to believe that rebellion against parental authority is a statutory requirement of the age, but this is not so. There is certainly a universal reaching for independence, but it need not carry angry or resentful overtones. One mother wrote, 'We had no problems at home, no rebellion. Of course we all adore each other, perhaps that's why.' Her children had met with opposition to their Christian standards at school, which made the bonds of home even stronger. The home can provide security and a quality of love which neither school nor peers can offer, and security and love are enormously important, not only to babies and to schoolchildren, but also to the teens. Close and warm relationships, cultivated from the cradle, can mean that when they are into their twenties your children can become your best friends.

All change

Over those years there are going to be many changes. Children change from beautiful bouncing babies that are

19

the focus of admiration to unnervingly awkward creatures that seem to upset people – creatures with bodies that bulge embarrassingly or with spindly knees and elbows that knock things flying. Parents change, finding themselves in the midst of another identity crisis as an empty nest comes into view. Fashions change. We just have to learn to accept that spiky hairstyles, deafening music and black leather trousers may not necessarily be morally wrong, even though distasteful – and avoid constantly nagging or carping. Too much negative criticism can break a child's spirit. St Paul advised, 'Do not provoke your teenager.'

Fashions change in bringing up children. The rigid clock watching for every feed has gone, but so has the extreme latitude of the last two decades. In *Baby and Child Care* Dr Spock has written, 'There should be firm leadership from a parent to make a child happier.' Yet we swing between the advocates of regulations and the school of go-as-you-please – and back again. Jeremy and Mavis have been much more strict in bringing up Samantha than their parents were with them. Samantha is not allowed ice-cream until her vegetables are eaten, she is not excused from the table till her parents have finished, whereas Jeremy used to run round the table during meals and hide underneath it, snatching his meal in between!

No matter how we change as the years go by, no matter which sort of regimen we choose, what really should be our top priority, from baby days, is the emotional tone of the home, and that this warm relationship should be maintained with the schoolchild and adolescent.

Problem parents

'Love is a special way of feeling.' Joan Walsh Anglund's charming little book gives sentimental descriptions of what this much abused word means. A better picture of what it really involves is given in 1 Corinthians 13 which makes it clear that where we love we also must be

20

prepared to endure. It has been summarised: 'Love is not just a nice thing you feel: it is a hard thing that you do.'

I have often wondered how Hannah felt when she handed over her little boy to Eli. She went home and stitched another little jacket that she could take to him next year. This touches the heart. Yet this was what love meant for her. It was the very best that she could do for him. She entrusted him to the representative of the God who had given him to her.

We may not be faced with the same hard choice, but in any event we need a realistic view of the child's real needs – security, stability, a firm hand with the loving heart. Love does not mean giving way to all the child's demands or buying endless gifts; it means, primarily, dependability and continuity of provision for physical and emotional needs. Parents are not all endowed with the same degree of capability in providing this vital stable framework for their children.

Wrapped in cotton wool

One of the basic needs of a child is to be allowed to grow up. This may sound obvious, yet there are some children whose natural urge to independence is restricted by an over-anxious mother or an over-protective father. There is a nice balance to be achieved between pushing a child before he is ready, and keeping him so wrapped in cotton wool that his independence is delayed. We must help our children to develop the courage and confidence that make for independence. At the same time we must teach them about moral courage – that it may be braver to refuse a rock climbing dare which would bring danger to others rather than to go ahead and do the rock-climbing. They may have to take a stand against sexual advances or smoking pot one day.

Children must be allowed freedom to experiment and to make their own mistakes, though we may hope that advice will help them to avoid them. Too much fussing becomes burdensome. When Adrian started to stay at school for his dinners his mother bothered about his dietary requirements. Every day she would ask, 'What did you have for dinner today, darling?' Adrian answered truthfully for a while. Then he got fed up with the inquisition and every day he answered the same – 'Sardines!' At last his puzzled mother went up to the school to complain. They had never had sardines!

Ugly duckling

'Even his mother said she wished he had never been born.' Tragically there are human children who, like Hans Andersen's duckling, are rejected by their mothers. Sometimes a difficult birth will produce an unnatural antipathy and the mother will not take to her baby; sometimes some childhood experience or emotional trauma is responsible. Sometimes there is, beneath the desire to reject the child, an equally strong yearning to establish a real relationship of love. Mary, a conscientious, warm-hearted Christian girl who was crossed in love before she met the man she married, could not accept her first-born son. When a little girl was born two years later Mary welcomed and took to her, still leaving the boy estranged. Andersen's perceptive story gives a graphic idea of the emotional pressure of such unhappiness. The duckling is of course, really a swan, but he grows up not knowing this. In the spring he sees two royal swans approaching him on the lake. He begs the beautiful birds to kill him because he is so ugly that he does not wish to live.

> 'Kill me,' said the poor bird; and he bent his head down to the surface of the water, and awaited death. But what did he see in the clear water below? His own image; no longer a dark grey bird, ugly and disagreeable to look at, but a graceful and beautiful swan.

The story of Mary's boy did have a happy ending, for with counselling she was able to find in her heart the love for him that deep down she longed to give. But some children do grow up in the shadow of rejection by one or even both parents. For them the love of Christ, when they find him, is especially wonderful, for it tells them that in God's sight there are no ugly ducklings. Each one of us is a swan.

Double bind

There are some mothers who have an ambivalent attitude towards their children. Outwardly they may appear loving and accepting towards the child but, underneath the veneer, there is a reservation. Perhaps the mother is a career woman and finds her child a liability, or perhaps he was not planned for nor wanted. She may be naturally a kind person and conscientious and so does her best according to her lights. But children are not so easily deceived where feelings are concerned. 'Of course Mummy loves you, only don't bother me now,' a mother shouts as she runs upstairs to dress for the theatre. So the poor child keeps getting reassuring messages of love from her words, but does not receive the love itself. Genuine love can be sensed instinctively by children, even if their parents are not demonstrative by nature. A parent with a divided attitude creates for the child a wounding emotional pressure.

Status symbols

Some parents feel that society is judging their performance as parents by the appearance, behaviour and attainments of their children. And so the child must be perfection in one way or another – in looks or manners or intelligence. Such children are never allowed to be themselves for 'Mummy is hurt' or 'Daddy is disappointed' if they do not come up to expectations. This is a sort of social blackmail that produces social rebels.

Black sheep

Sometimes parents are afraid that a child will take after some undesirable relative, especially if looks are similar. 'You'll turn out bad like your Uncle Joe, and land up in prison and disgrace us all.' They watch every little thing he does and may be more ready to punish him than they would otherwise be because of this fear. It is true that beneath this severity there may be hidden the love that makes for such anxiety, but nonetheless the child lives under the shadow of watchful disapproval.

Why are they shouting at each other?

It is easy to underestimate how adult problems can affect children. Even though they do not understand business affairs and money problems, they are perfectly capable of knowing that a shouting match means trouble, or of interpreting sour looks and hostile silences. It shakes a child's security to see mummy and daddy cross with each other. However, something can be usefully salvaged if they can also see a genuine loving making up. They can see that love is stronger than anger and that the framework of love holds, which is immensely reassuring. They are also given a pattern of behaviour in forgiving and making up, and, in the forgiveness which their parents extend to each other they can see a striking illustration of the forgiveness of God towards us.

Putting old heads on young shoulders

One of the most disastrous legacies of this adult generation is the fact that parents have lost confidence in themselves. The general lowering of moral standards has left them shaken, the advances of science have confused their ideas of right and wrong; as a nation we have lost our hold on religious belief. Many children are therefore without moral guidelines. The weight of making enormous decisions is on their shoulders, but they are without the necessary criteria to form rational judgements for they have not been given the standards, values and principles of previous generations. They must simply make personal choices on the grounds of expediency. Parents have even taken refuge in the idea that children know best what is right for them. Feeble platitudes have replaced considered parental guidance: 'I don't want my child indoctrinated with religion. He can make up his own mind when he is grown up,' or, 'I don't mind her having sex as long as she has a meaningful relationship with the boy.' Parents who opt out do not make life easy for the young – they put a burden on their shoulders.

Now for the good news

It may seem depressing to look at the negative side of family relationships in this way, but nonetheless it is useful to do so, for if we are aware of pitfalls we can take steps to avoid them. There are no perfect parents and no perfect children. We are all different and we all make mistakes. This is in itself an encouragement, for we can look around and see how 'normally' the vast majority of children grow up, no matter the pains of doing so. A child brought up with no stresses and strains would be a peculiar child, and indeed some pressures are not only normal, they are essential.

It is quite possible that the next generation of parents will be more capable, for they have opportunities to become better informed about what parenthood involves and can see that it is not a bed of roses without thorns, that some difficulties are to be expected. Owing to psychological research we know much more about the development of children than ever before, and what is known soon becomes common knowledge through numerous media channels. Psychiatrists and social workers and media 'aunts' who bring all sorts of family problems before the public view, have made it easier to talk about them and to find help.

We need to consider home-making as important a career as any of the professions, and to include in a programme of education for parenthood the basic skills of running a home, such as budgeting, cooking, hygiene, first aid, and the dietary needs of a family. In addition there should be an initial course in child development, as parents and teachers need to know about growing children, the difficulties they may encounter and sources of advice and help. This may sound ambitious, but in fact home-making should be given serious, even priority consideration, for it is an essential factor in the building of a nation.

You are being watched

Your influence as a parent is probably at its strongest when you are not making a conscious effort to teach anything. It is, for example, no good trying to teach a child about the love of God unless you demonstrate that love in your attitude towards him. A loving parent provides a visual aid of God's love, which also serves the child as a pattern for his own behaviour towards the children he may one day have. It is often without any conscious intention that adults, parents in particular, mould children. These lines, from *Polestar*, put it in a nutshell:

A child who lives with criticism learns to criticise.
A child who lives with hostility learns to fight.
A child who lives with ridicule learns to be shy.
A child who lives with shame learns to feel guilt.
A child who lives with tolerance learns to be patient.
A child who lives with encouragement learns confidence.
A child who lives with fairness learns justice.
A child who lives with praise learns to appreciate.
A child who lives with security learns to have faith.
A child who lives with approval learns to like itself.
A child who lives with acceptance and friendship learns to find love in the world.

Throughout their growing years children are engaged in the task of establishing who they are and what their role in life is to be. Small children will copy whatever the parent who happens to be present is doing – watering the garden, painting a chair, making a cake, but gradually he or she begins to take on the patterns of behaviour of the same sex parent. Three-year-old Emily, like most little girls, loves to have a dolls' tea-party and to do the washing up in a bowl – a task that she will probably find less enchanting later! She is modelling herself on her mother. This is an important step in establishing a sense of identity, and a clear view of sex roles is helpful to a child in discovering his or her own self. The current craze for 'unisex' clothes and hairstyles, the playing down of sex differences and the presentation of homosexuality and lesbianism as natural, hinder the adolescent at a critical stage in his search for identity. This is the central problem of this stage of life, for the adolescent who does not develop a strong hold on who he is and what his role in society is to be, is left with a sense of diffusion which may involve suicidal tendencies or other neuroses. In family life the sex-roles based on the biblical view of man are the most likely to give the child a strong basis for his self-image.

The child will also build his self-image on those he loves and admires, and to this end will seek patterns among those close to him, or from pop or film stars or characters in fiction. One eight-year-old, locked in the bathroom as a punishment, thought to herself, 'Now what would Robin Hood do in this situation?' Parents play a crucial role in providing the most significant and influential role models. You may not realise it, but you are being watched – watched when you keep your temper and when you lose it, watched when you read your Bible or pray or react to bad news. You are giving your child a picture of the person he will one day be, unless he rejects what he sees. Adolescents often go through a stage of reacting against their parents' model and will dress and behave in a style as different as possible. 'I don't know who I am, but it certainly ain't going to be like you,' they seem to be saying. Yet they will be surprisingly like you in middle age.

There are many things that we have to pass on by instruction, but values are largely modelled. This is important to remember as children grow up and are at an age at which they no longer like to be told what to do. We can teach children to read and introduce them to Bible notes; but a love for the Bible is something which we will pass on by our own attitude towards it.

Neither can we make personal decisions of faith for our children. It is notoriously counter-productive to try to pressurise teenagers into Christian commitment. To attempt it is a sure way of modelling hypocrisy rather than faith. But I have always remembered my father standing rather too near a window during an air-raid, and I was afraid for him. I called to him to come away, and he did so to please me, but unhurriedly, quietly filling his pipe and quoting 'Be still, and know that I am God.'

As children grow towards independence we have to learn to let them go their own way, but nonetheless they will continue to learn from our attitudes towards, for instance, money and success. Teenagers are quick to spot inconsistency, if, for instance, we are telling them to 'take no thought for the morrow' and yet driving ourselves into ulcers or nervous breakdowns with anxiety about finance or ambition.

Parents as providers

The extent to which parents are able to provide for the physical, intellectual, emotional and spiritual needs of their children will make a major difference to the way in which they are able to cope with the pressures of life as they grow up.

The immediate and widespread results of material deprivation in the famine stricken areas of the world are too sadly obvious on our TV screens, but real poverty on a smaller scale has nonetheless devastating effects on the children who suffer. In this country, during the last century, philanthropists such as Dr Barnardo and Lord Shaftesbury found their hearts touched by starving orphans and children abandoned because their parents were unable to provide for them, and began their worthy enterprises. Now there are many caring institutions ready to take up those who fall through the net of the welfare state.

Poverty, neglect and malnutrition make children prematurely aged, if indeed they survive at all. Henry Mayhew, the Victorian social historian, noted this effect in his book *London Labour and the London Poor* (1851), where he writes of his meeting with a little watercress seller:

> Although only eight years of age, she had entirely lost all childish ways and was in thought and manner, a woman . . . Her little face, pale and thin with privation, was wrinkled where the dimples ought to have been and she would sigh frequently.

This aging effect can be seen in the sad eyes which look out from wizened faces brought to us by television from Bangladesh and Ethiopia. We are condemnatory of Victorian society and saddened but not surprised by the condition of children overseas, but the plain truth is that according to Child Poverty Action there are cases of such deprivation in this country at this time. In their recently produced journal on nutrition they reveal the nature and extent of the pressure which malnutrition is having on children, here and now.

Provision for the mind

Equally important is the provision that parents make for the mind. The early language experience and learning environment of the home will have a profound influence on their child's intellectual development, communicative skills, ability to make friends and also on other aspects of personality such as confidence and outgoingness. Children who have not had the stimulation that they need are at a disadvantage when they enter school and limp along behind the others. They may become socially inept and unsure of themselves or even join the surprising number of adults who cannot read. They suffer the pressure of living in a society where literacy counts for much in wage-

29

earning ability and status. It begins with the communication in the cot. Even the smallest babies need to know that their mothers and fathers have something to say to them; the bedtime story, looking at books and pictures can be marvellous times of sharing the ideas and thoughts which can only take real shape in the process of framing language. Books are an even more important part of the nursery scene than the well-loved animals, dolls and toys. Television can be a hindrance to language development if a child is left in front of it alone indefinitely, but it can also be a positive help if you sit alongside and chat about some appropriate programme. We tend to assume that children see what is before their eyes; but the fact is that we all see much more clearly the things that we talk about. When they start to draw trees, children nearly always draw something that looks like a lollipop. A student on teaching practice talked with the children who gathered round her during break. They stood under a tree in the playground and quite incidentally began to talk about the dappling shadows of the leaves, the formation of the branches and the twigs, the texture of the bark and the shape of the mighty oak. Later she noticed that their drawings of trees were lifelike, with leaves and twigs and shadows, instead of the previous potted versions.

I sometimes hear mothers dismiss the myriad questions that the child keeps asking. But children's questions must be taken seriously, even those that are too difficult for us, because in answering we can teach them to analyse what is going on around them and also build a resistance to advertising pressures. In encouraging children to talk about all different aspects of their experience you are teaching them to handle ideas, to think. A youngster who can think rationally will be able to sift the arguments of political activists, scientologists, cults, and test them against scriptural truth.

The spiritual 'climate' of the home

The ethos of the home is a powerful influence in the nurturing of spiritual life. If we hope to convey the message that Christ understands our children's fears and failures, their problems and panics, then that is the quality of understanding that we must extend to our children. If we want them to believe that God listens to their prayers, then we must listen to all that they are longing to say.

There is a difference between 'religious' homes, where the rules are laid down in a legalistic, rather daunting way, and Christian homes where order flows from the fruit of the Spirit and where there are lovely things to do together, that give scope to the child's God-given creativity. We always need to be wary lest our fervent hopes for our children should become an off-putting pressure of the sort that turns children against religion. However, boys and girls brought up in Christian homes by a Christian mum and dad, with the Bible at the breakfast table and prayers at night, will be likely to find that Christian commitment will be a natural step for them in their own time.

Important though the Bible and prayers are, it is even more important that children should be able to see that their parents put Christ first in their lives; that as well as being committed to Christ they are committed to each other; that in spite of the inevitable occasional disagreements they intend to stay together; that their love for Christ comes out in the way they treat each other and the little everyday things that they do for each other. It is sometimes very easy to ignore or forget the spiritual dimension to life in the mundane affairs of every day, yet that is just where we should be looking, so that we can help our children to be aware of the way in which God is working out his purposes, both in the world at large and also in our individual lives.

A home where there is a real spiritual dimension is a home where there is 'love, joy, peace, longsuffering,

gentleness, goodness, faith, meekness, temperance'
(Galatians 5.22–3 AV). Even when an adolescent in his
struggle for autonomy, rejects the institutional church,
these attributes of Christ himself will still keep his admiration. We hope that our children will remain loyal to the
church but most of all we long for them to follow Christ
throughout their lives.

Influence and pressure

There is a difference between influence and pressure.
We cannot avoid having an influence on our children.
Influence implies unconscious or willing modelling:
pressure implies some degree of forcing and resistance.
But in some cases, pressure may, however, not be a bad
thing. Not *all* pressure is damaging and some pressures
are very necessary.

In any home there must inevitably be pressures as the
child reaches each new stage of development, and there
will be conflicts with authority as he tries to establish his
autonomy and become an independent person. There are
constant small battles throughout the growing years, but
they usually reach certain peaks. For example there are
the 'terrible twos'. The two-year-old is determined to
prove his power and to find his limits, that is, to see how
far he can go in getting his own way and how much aggro
his parents will take. This is how he learns who he is and
learns to become independent. Joanna used to say 'Let
me do it *my own self*', fiercely struggling with buttons and
bows. Peter will fly into a rage if he is given his clothes
instead of choosing them himself, and is determined to
dress himself no matter how long it takes. Again at
adolescence these battles reach a peak – the final conflicts
of tentative maturity. It is through these battles of the
will that a child brings his personality into being; they are
a necessary part of growing up.

However, that does not mean that we must allow
ourselves to be blackmailed by fear of what the neighbours will think. There may be some occasions on which

it will be right to give way, but it is important that parents should establish their authority while the children are small. Later it is nearly impossible. Letting things slide may be an easy course, but it does not help character development. A child needs to know that there is someone in control. This does not of course apply to absolutely all occasions. When a child is tired or not feeling well it is wise to pass some things over, but as a general principle in the running of the home it is helpful for a child to feel the pressure of authority keeping things stable. All good parents exert pressure as well as influence, but it needs sensitivity and discrimination to know whether the pressure is pressure of the right sort.

4

Discipline and Parental Ambition

Discipline your son in his early years while there is hope.
If you don't you will ruin his life . . .
If you refuse to discipline your son it proves you don't love him.
King Solomon

'Don't stand up in the boat', said Daddy. They were out
in a rowing boat on a family holiday, mother and father
and two children – just a typical united, loving family. It
was at that time when there was a strong reaction against
putting any pressure on children to obey. The current
philosophy in child-rearing was that initiatives should
come from the children and that any imposed sanctions
on their natural desires might result in harmful inhibitions.

'Don't stand up, Sonia,' said Daddy again. But Sonia
did stand up, and the little boat rocked and swayed
uncontrollably.

'*Sit down!*' shouted Daddy loudly and anxiously as he
felt the balance going. And Sonia laughed and jumped
up and down and over they all went, mother and father
and two children into the deep blue sea.

Daddy was able to save Sonia and the others, but he
himself was drowned. It is a true story, and Sonia will
live with that memory and that guilt for all her days.

All children need to learn to obey for their own safety
and that of others. They need discipline, because it is the
only way to learn self-control. They need it because it
involves respect for others; it is part and parcel of
acknowledging authority and conforming socially and it is
associated with acquiring a conscience.

Inhibitions

Yes, discipline does mean pressure – but it is a necessary pressure. Society would have lost its cohesion long ago if parents had abandoned their attempts to persuade children to conform and so to become good citizens. Down the centuries parents have found different ways of persuading children to do so – some of them quite horrifying.

Some Puritan writers held the threat of hell-fire over the heads of their infants. One Victorian author, Mrs Sherwood, gave a terrible warning in the form of a story in which children who have quarrelled are taken to see the decaying body, hanging on a gibbet, of a man who had murdered his brother in a fit of anger. We remember, too, Dickens' picture of Mr Murdstone thrashing David Copperfield – 'He beat me then as if he would have beaten me to death.' These methods do not appeal to us today!

Many of our current ideas concerning the upbringing of children go back to an eighteenth century philosopher, Jean Jacques Rousseau, who did not believe in punishment, but in allowing children to learn from their mistakes. For example, a boy who had broken a window would have had to suffer the effects of the cold winter weather whistling round his head while he slept. Rousseau's ideas have had considerable influence on educational thinking, bringing a greater emphasis on the child's own experience and view of life, and a relaxation of severity in upbringing. Undoubtedly this has had its beneficial aspects: but combined with other factors such as the general lowering of moral standards, it has contributed towards making the word 'inhibition' a dirty word. Obedience, considerate manners and even ethical conduct no longer hold so universally acknowledged a place as they formerly did in raising children.

Perhaps it is time we realised that not all inhibitions are bad. We are seeing the results of the 'Swinging Sixties'; children who were brought up without inhibitions are now raising rootless children to indulge their unbridled fancies in hooliganism, vandalism and violence. Without the restriction of accepted codes of conduct life becomes a free-for-all where the weakest go to the wall.

Recipe for disaster

We have come to feel rather guilty about punishing children, or even about denying their wishes. But a child may suffer as much from too lenient a control as from too harsh a one. There are times in all homes when we have to turn a blind eye – maybe mother is in hospital – but a child who is never corrected is a deprived child. He is being systematically fed with the idea that there are no limits, that he can do just as he likes with no regard for others. He is bound to get into trouble when friends come along with bright ideas for making themselves a nuisance on their motorbikes in some seaside town or starting a riot at a football match.

> We don't know what to do with our daughter, who is barely fourteen years old. She wants to stay out really late with older friends and go to places that I would really rather not have her go, but we are afraid if we say too much she will get rebellious and turn against us. How shall we deal with her?

This letter to Billy Graham in *The Christian Herald* is typical of a home where children have reached an age when they want to feel grown up and be free from restrictions. Many parents face this dilemma. People sometimes think that given unlimited freedom children will develop an inner discipline of their own. The opposite is more generally true. Without the control we impose on them, children do not learn to discipline themselves. And without self-discipline, with no control over their own impulses, even a knowledge of right and wrong will not prevent their being in grave danger from the pressure of the world – not only the more obvious ones of sex, drugs and alcohol, but also of being manipulated by anyone who hopes to take advantage of them.

In his reply Billy Graham says that their daughter has had too little experience of life to know what is best for her. Out of their very love for her the parents must take the risk of rebellion that they fear. The alternative of letting her do anything she likes is an even greater risk and she might 'end up in deep trouble'. He pointed out that a habit of falling in with parents' wishes needed to be started before this point is reached.

Keeping a balance

Even if we all agree that discipline is important we would still doubtless have different ideas of what it means and of how to achieve it. The word itself carries harsh associations of soldiers on parade, but, rather than some rigid system, we should aim for a pattern of living in an atmosphere of affection and security. With the background of a loving home children usually want to please their parents, and the basis of the discipline should be that desire.

There should be few rules, and they should be obeyed because they are based on common sense. For example, children should always let their parents know if they are going out to play with a friend, and they should return at the stated time. This is vital since we live with the menace of child molesting and other such horrors. We have to balance concern for safety with allowance for children to exercise their initiative and grow in independence. For this reason, it is best not to be rigid over things that are not really important. You can then be consistent about those that matter while giving the child the opportunity to make some choices and decisions. A balance must be kept between conformity and the child's need to express individuality.

Handling them right

The way in which we control our children is a very personal thing. It has to be worked out as part of the whole complex adjustment of family relationships.

If it is at all possible it is best to avoid punishment. This is more likely to be possible where control arises naturally out of good parent-child relationships. It is the same in a school. Where discipline is working you do not notice it. In a happy environment children want to do the right thing; they seek the praise that builds up their self-image, the creation of which is the central task of childhood. 'I am a responsible/unselfish/kind/helpful boy – or girl.'

It has been shown that reward is a far more effective means of training than punishment, and praise is more powerful than any material reward. Unfortunately some of us are natural punishers rather than natural rewarders! A child who is fairly confident of his ability to win approval behaves in a more relaxed fashion than a child whose fear of punishment makes him nervous. The confident child can make rational choices, and given a few bouts of mischief or contrariness, will develop in harmony. No one wants children who behave like puppets. Parents can then respond without over-indulgence or over-strictness. A child's rights should be respected, not in the political sense, but because of his God-given free spirit. Appropriate rules and manners should be taught when he is at an age to understand and see their reason.

Although father is the head of the household, mother is the heart of it, and a tremendous amount depends on her management. Good management means few punishments. She needs to pre-empt the causes of bad behaviour: boredom, overtiredness and hunger make children irritable; wet days bring frustration, and plenty of puzzles and indoor games are needed, with opportunities to let off steam. You need to be tactful when a child seems listless. I have found that the day after I had to be cross with a child he would go down with some illness that I had not realised he was sickening for.

We should also take into account a child's motives. Sometimes what appears as naughtiness arises from a natural even laudable desire to do things 'my own self.' Determination is a fine character trait which should not be crushed. The handling of a child should be related to his individual personality, not to any preconceived ideas of what he 'ought to be', and similar offences cannot always be treated in the same way, for a sensitive child might be emotionally damaged by a punishment that another could take in his stride. Another child's need might be for a firm, even rather authoritarian type of control.

There is bound to come a time, however, when parents will have to decide what they will do about flagrant disobedience. It is as well to have thought about this beforehand, and to let the children know what to expect. In such cases, and since we are trying to teach them self-discipline, we too should use self-control and try to avoid the angry outburst that can be frightening. But a parent who explodes can also make up with a similar outpouring of affection. As Jean Watson has put it, 'If you are a shouter, you need to be a hugger and kisser.'

Children around the age of eight or nine are in the process of developing a moral sense and mind very much about the fairness of the way they are treated. It is important to consider whether their misdemeanour was a mistake, a mischievous prank, or wilful disobedience, and whether it violated some important principle, perhaps involving safety, and therefore needs a lesson that will be remembered. A punishment must be seen to be just.

Sarcasm is totally inappropriate to use with any age of child, for it undermines self-esteem, which is the very trait that we should be doing all in our power to build. Nor do I think that it is fair to use a sort of emotional blackmail. 'It makes Mummy very sad' should not be given as a reason for condemning some activity – things are wrong simply because they are wrong. Playing on a child's feelings can leave them overloaded with guilt. Children do anyway feel guilty when they have done wrong, especially children of Christian homes who may develop an acute awareness of sinfulness that could later become neurotic. A seven-year-old, left to watch his baby sister on the bed for a brief while, left her side and she tumbled on the floor, fortunately unhurt; but he was overcome with remorse. 'I'll kill myself,' he wept.

Since children are so different it is sometimes a good idea to make the punishment not only fit the crime, but also the child. A range of possibilities could include a ban on sweets; the carrying out of some task in the house or garden for example, washing the car, cleaning shoes, weeding, washing up; a curfew on time with friends; withholding some treat or outing; docking of pocket money, and finally – most controversial of all – corporal punishment.

A sharp whack?

The phrase 'corporal punishment' arouses strong emotions, yet it simply means punishment to the body and so could mean anything from a light smack with the hand to a caning. Opinions range from those who would outlaw its use in any form, to those for whom it is the biblical answer for behavioural problems. A friend told me:

> My wife and I are firm believers in spanking. I think I can honestly say that neither of us have ever hit our children in anger. All smacks were administered in love by parents who loved the child. The Bible's teaching, experience as a father, and twenty-five years as a pastor, visitor and counsellor have convinced me that if there is one single secret to the successful upbringing of children, it is the correct use of corporal punishment.

Apparently it has even been used effectively with young adolescents:

> Over the last few months I have seen or heard of at least seven younger teenagers who have been a great trial to their parents – defiant and disobedient. I have noted what had

happened to these seven teenagers. Four of the children have received corporal punishment in some form or other and the problems ceased thereafter. Two did not receive any corporal punishment and the problem is continuing. The seventh child has been warned by his mother that he is not too old to receive it and he has improved his behaviour tremendously.

I don't believe it is true to the teaching of Scripture to ignore times when children are being deliberately disobedient, defiant, refusing to do what they are told. It seems to me that here we have an obligation to correct them, and those of us who believe that the Bible is true and that it clearly teaches that there is a use for corporal punishment in the bringing up of children, do not go on to believe that we shall spend all our days spanking them. Frankly, it is not like that. I often think that it is a case of a spank in time saves nine. People who wait too long before they correct a child let the fault get ingrained.

Not all parents would agree:

Our experience of using corporal punishment is that apart from slaps when children are very young, it can become simply a release of a parent's frustrations. It is usually counterproductive to the development of a trusting friendship which grows deeper over the years. It has proved better to take time to talk and explain and encourage than to try to exert an unexplained authority (Colin and Beryl Selby in *Christian Arena*).

These parents severally are of course dealing with different children. Maybe the children who responded so well to corporal punishment were the sort of active extrovert children who would anyway have preferred a quick whack to a long talk. Maybe the children who were open to persuasion were more amenable by nature. We do not know. Nor do we know about the personality differences of their parents. In any event those parents who whack and those who discuss must equally have thought about it beforehand, even perhaps among other issues contem-

41

plated during the days of their engagement, and look for and expect God's help in deciding what is right for their own family.

My own experience has convinced me that the behaviour of children depends to a quite extraordinary extent on what you confidently assume it is going to be. I have found that where you are able to communicate (without words) the belief that you are expecting a certain response, it follows. If you are dithery and all worked up you may expect trouble. If you know (in spite of appearances) in your heart that these children are co-operative and law-abiding, they will be. I understand that lion-tamers have found the same!

It gets particularly tough for parents when children reach teenage – if you give them too much freedom they feel insecure; if you give them too little they feel restricted. It's a problem to know how far you can exert pressure on them in order to keep them from serious temptations and dangers. Furthermore they are themselves in two minds about growing up. They long to be mature. They strive to be independent. At the same time they can be overawed both by adult society and also by the pressure of their friends. Longfellow has described the adolescent girl:

> Standing with reluctant feet
> Where the brook and river meet.

They do not know how to handle situations when many voices are clamouring to make them do something that in their hearts they fear or do not wish to do. Then it can be a relief to have a strict dad who says 'No'. You can save your son or daughter a lot of embarrassment if you turn yourself into a sort of Mr Barrett of Wimpole Street on occasion. You may be surprised by the relief which greets your refusal to allow the house to be used for a party in your absence, or when you forbid a visit to a seedy disco. However, at this age they should be given credit for some commonsense and responsibility.

Knowing your reasons for refusal and knowing what might be the consequences, both in terms of possible danger and of certain punishment, they can make informed choices. A friend of my childhood gave evidence of decision-making ability when he climbed onto the roof of the school chapel and decorated the spire with a 'bedroom article'! He knew he would be caned. It was worth it, he said. True to character – he became a commando!

Self-discipline and success

Children who have been brought up with habits of self-discipline have a better hope of getting through examinations or achieving on the field of sport, and of coping with the competitive world of business or profession when they leave school. I heard Alicia Markova, speaking on the radio, say 'I was a very obedient child. If I was asked to do something I never said "I can't." I would always say, "I'll try" and I would go ahead and try, and by trying something happened . . . A thing one hardly dare say nowadays – to ask a child to be obedient.' No one reaches the top in any walk of life without self-discipline. A teacher has written:

> Such discipline however does not just happen. It needs to be taught in the home and in the classroom. At first it has to be imposed from outside, but, wisely and lovingly given, it will lead gradually to a self-imposed discipline in the teenager and young adult. The attitude that doing what I feel like brings happiness is unfortunately also taught by parents who are either over-indulgent or are having so many problems in their own relationship that the effort to discipline is too much. This lack of discipline often leads to poor achievement with consequent low self-esteem and unpopularity. It contributes to the sad picture of bored, frustrated, under-achieving and attention-seeking teenagers who disrupt school and later society (*ACT NOW*).

Children who lack self-control are neither happy nor popular. Their frenetic behaviour invites teasing but loses friends. On the other hand the very effort of self-control gives a child the feeling of self-worth. One of the greatest joys of parenthood is that of seeing our children happy and making good. We are justified in exerting this type of pressure on them; but only in relation to their personal fulfilment and not to any material success that it may bring, nor to any reflected glory that may come to us. There is all the difference in the world between taking an encouraging interest in their activities and putting the wrong sort of pressure on them, so that the effort to succeed becomes a strain and they get the feeling that they are never good enough.

Our ambitions for our kids

Most parents are ambitious for their children in the sense that they have hopes for them. What are those hopes? Some of us would like to see our children following in our footsteps, maybe in the arts, or on the stage, or in a profession or family business. This is fine provided the child has both the innate ability and the desire to do so. But however hard-working he may be he may still not have what it takes to succeed in our chosen path, and however obedient, his choice in life may be quite different from ours.

A student who fails his exams is burdened not only with his own disappointment but also with that of his parents, and with guilt because he feels that he has let them down. Kenneth is a conscientious hard-working medical student, very fond of his parents and eager to please them. One evening he telephoned his student health doctor in a state of great anxiety. He had had to break the news at home that he had failed some important examination. Instead of receiving sympathy and support from his parents, his father had given him a dressing down. 'You're making your mother ill,' he had said. The combination of failure and self-reproach that such an attitude engenders can undermine a person's confidence, not only in his ability, but in his personal worth. Some of us are not able to give our children all that we would have liked, but we shall have given them something of priceless value if we have got it into their heads and hearts that examination results and school successes, however pleasing, have nothing to do with their worth as human beings. They are precious because of who they are, not because of what they have done or can do.

The competitive instinct is part of our human nature, and the striving to outdo all the others starts young. 'Go in and win!' we say. 'Win! Win!' Tamar was four. She was very excited when her parents went to see her in her first dancing display. Very sweet she looked in her pink leotard and tights, with her hair tied up tight like a ballerina.

'Was I the best?' she asked her mother afterwards.

'You were very good indeed,' said her mother. 'You were quite lovely.'

'But was I the *best?*' persisted Tamar. 'Daddy said I was the *best*.'

Parents' ambitions for the young also start very early and have a strong pressurising influence, often through the giving of rewards for school successes. 'Mummy has promised to take me to the ballet if I come top at the end of term,' I have heard, or 'Daddy says he will give me a wristwatch/bicycle/pony if I get through my exams'. The child who is disappointed by a poor result then suffers the additional disappointment of losing the gift as well; while the winner gets the impression that everything can be measured in material terms. Failure carries overtones of disapproval that can be diminishing, while both success and failure then imply that the parents' estimate of their child depends on his ability – for presents always suggest love and approval.

Some parents are particularly ambitious for their children to succeed in those areas where they themselves had great hopes but no success. For example, the cricket fanatic who was never able to make his name in cricket and is therefore determined that his son shall do so. *Never*

45

try to live out your failed dreams through your children.
There is nothing better that you can do for them than to
dedicate them to God for the whole of their lives; to teach
them to trust his plan for their lives whether in success or
failure. We need to learn the truth of Romans 8.28 as
early as possible – that God works in everything, failure
as well as success, for the good of those who love him.

Help your children to understand that while you are
interested in everything they do, your love for them is
not affected by what they are able to accomplish. John
was a pre-clinical student evacuated from London during
the blitz. At that time one of the pop songs the soldiers
were singing was, 'It's a lovely day tomorrow.' Struggling
hard with his work under these difficult conditions, John
was shattered by the news that he had failed an important
exam. He sent home a telegram: 'Failed Second MB.
Home tomorrow. Love John.' Back came the reply: 'It's
a lovely day tomorrow. Love Mum and Dad.' This
message of love not only encouraged him then, but has
since helped many students he has counselled during his
long career as a student health physician.

Like Hannah, we do the best for our children when we
put them in the hands of God, trusting that his perfect
plan for them may be just as likely to operate through
what humanly speaking may appear to be failure as
through what humanly speaking may appear to be success.

46

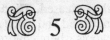

5

Worlds Apart

Teach a child to choose the right path,
and when he is older he will remain on it.
King Solomon

Children spend a large part of their waking day in school, and its influence is likely to be deep and long-lasting. Many children start at nursery school nowadays, and may continue till eighteen – that is a lot of schooling, covering all the most impressionable years.

Right paths

The right school is immensely important. A child needs to be in a school suited both to his ability and personality in order to fulfil his real potential and acquire the moral fibre necessary to resist undesirable pressures. The type of school carries significance for adult life and career choice; the difference between formality or freedom will affect attitudes and behaviour patterns; the quality of teaching, the staff, friends and peer pressures, will all be influences on achievement and personality formation; and the ethos of the school together with the relative value of the religious education will either nurture spiritual awareness or drive him into scepticism.

Most children will go through the state system; but within it schools vary widely, depending on the area, the size of the school, the Head and the staff. Some children will be sent to boarding-school and become habituated to the rule of authority – that is, unless it turns them into rebels. A ballet school is a world of its own, with its own structured discipline and its specialised values. Very different would be a school organised on the lines advocated by A.S. Neil, where at one time pupils might attend

47

lessons or not as they pleased. There are schools where every minute is timetabled and games are organised, and there are village schools where children get their exercise by tumbling about in the playground or climbing trees in the paddock. There are single sex schools which may influence a child's sexual orientation and boy-girl relationships; there are church schools and schools where a religious foundation still counts for something; there are highly academic schools; politically conscious schools; free-for-all schools with violence in the playground.

We must remember that pressures from within the school meet whatever the child already has within by virtue of inherited characteristics and the influence of home. So that although the type of school exerts its own pressures, that does not mean that all the children from the same school will turn out like sausages. Every child, whether destined to become a leader or not, will one day play a part in society. In so far as their education will exert its moulding influence on all of them, teachers, even of the youngest children, have to accept responsibility for having a hand in the shaping of society. Absolutely fundamental to our whole educational system must be the belief that each child matters.

Pattern for life

Pat Leach runs a creche in the Moss Side Precinct in Manchester, two hundred yards from where the 1981 riot took place. It offers children from many different cultural backgrounds an environment in which they can freely integrate with the local children, learning to conform to a society in which many faiths and cultures play a part. Later in life this early experience should be an antidote to the poisonous pressure of racial antagonism. And, for the present, mothers and children alike are relieved of the pressures inherent in the neighbourhood situation where a shifting population resides on large council estates and where play facilities are few and busy roads make outdoor play unsafe.

Pat, of Jamaican origin but born locally, sings in her church choir. Her Jamaican husband works for the Greater Manchester Youth Association. She sees the initial entry into the educational system as of vital importance, not for the intellectual benefits but for the personal values:

> The creche has a much more important job than just minding children. By surrounding them with love and affection and creating a stimulating environment we hope they will thrive and develop. The way under-fives are treated sets a pattern for their lives. Parents don't need lots of money, or expensive toys or gadgets to give children the needed stimuli. Cardboard boxes, plastic bottles, margarine tubs, clothes pegs will do.

In her opinion the pressures which turn children into delinquents arise from the breakdown of family life. Her advice and support for mothers help to relieve those marital problems which often end in disaster. She is 'convinced' that the preservation of the family unit is of high priority, that most of the problems of personal psychology or of crime and violence, are due to the breakdown of the family or its inadequacy. She is sure that the spirit she and her assistants create in the creche can radiate through the neighbourhood and contribute towards the development of a healthier, happier society.

Nursery schools provide a valuable extension of the world of a child. They are a safety valve for overwrought mothers who feel inadequate for the demands of motherhood or who need to go out to work. At the same time, they relieve pressures on the children who might otherwise suffer physical or emotional abuse. However, nursery school may not necessarily be the best answer for all. A sensitive child may find the parting from mother and the experience of socialisation traumatic. He may be too young to cope with the demands of two different worlds. There are dangers in introducing a new authority figure to a child whose own parents are inadequate or uncaring; where a happy parent-child relationship has not been established it is confusing to a child, in the process of modelling his identity, when a strange authority appears on the scene.

We need to encourage parents to carry authority competently and assume the traditional role of parenthood. Max Patterson, the Scots psychologist, has said that 'approved schools are stuffed to the doors with children who had not found authority in their parents.'

Playgroups keep mothers and children together, easing loneliness or boredom, and many churches make this a valuable part of ministry to the housebound or single parent. Mothers invited to help feel themselves valued and gain confidence in running the home and raising the children. Trained playground leaders advise them on imaginative activities which they can manage in the home; a caring mother may provide a richer language experience for her toddler, chatting about the pots and pans he turns out of the cupboard, than a teacher who has to provide for a roomful of children, however well equipped. As such, the relationship between a busy teacher and pupil may not be the most effective one to encourage the total development of a child at this age. We are in danger of expecting too much from teachers and undervaluing the role of caring parents.

Living in two worlds

When children reach the age of four or five parents must decide what they are going to do about schooling. Their choice is not entirely free. They are under certain constraints – the area where they live, their financial situation, perhaps their religious denomination and later the intellectual ability of the child. Many parents are aware that the ethos and attitudes of the school their child attends will affect his whole life and this is a question that causes them much thought and anxiety.

When a child is obviously unhappy or under-achieving and consultation with the Head brings no improvement, the only solution may be a change of school. This is not a light decision, but where the trouble arises from a personality clash with a teacher it is essential to remove the child from the spirit-crushing pressure.

Sometimes a child may have to attend a school which his parents do not wholeheartedly approve. Sometimes he may find himself living in two worlds. For many children the world of school is a totally different place from the world of home. There are different standards and values, different attitudes and behaviour, different moral codes and beliefs. A different sort of language may be spoken. This may make it hard for the child to achieve a unified view of life and to develop a satisfactory picture of himself as a whole person: 'I am this person at home and that person at school.' And this may be true. A child who throws his weight about at home may be orderly and conforming under the discipline of school. Or a child who is disruptive in the classroom may be retiring or even responsible when he gets back to a home where is expected to undertake certain tasks, maybe looking after a younger sibling. A different environment makes for a different person.

On the other hand, the school environment can exert heavy pressure on a child to fall in with its ways and prevailing philosophy. In a secular society this is very likely to make Christian children uncomfortably conspicuous, both for what they believe and for how they behave.

Hostile environment

A vicar told me of one of his parishioners whose daughter 'certainly gets a fair amount of mickey-taking because she is a believing and practising Christian'. He continued:

> She seems to be standing up to it, but going back home I think there have been occasions when there have been tears, when she has cried because the situation has been so difficult. But her parents have prayed with her and encouraged her and helped her, and with the fellowship of the local church

she is succeeding in standing firm under the difficulties which exist. You can keep your eyes on your children when they are at home but when at school they must sort out their own problems and there is very little you can do. A parent who spends all his time on the phone to the head teacher, complaining about what other children are doing to theirs, is not at the end of the day going to be very helpful to them.

Children at boarding school are most vulnerable because they cannot go home to their parents at the end of the day for prayers and encouragement. Parents who are called abroad face a difficult decision. The son of Ruanda missionaries used to wait for the boots to come whistling through the dormitory at his head, as he knelt by his bed to pray. A twelve-year-old, newly arrived at one of our leading public schools, had lemonade and other less pleasant liquid poured over his head when he was converted during his first term. The school chaplain and his wife made a home from home for those enduring such martyrdom; but they found it a problem to know how to help without inviting reprisals on the victims.

Although tormented by their peers, at one time Christian children would have found their principles and beliefs upheld by the school authorities. This may not be so now. As morning prayers disappear and RE loses its Christian thrust, schools are following the drift of society in becoming increasingly secular. Life in such schools is likely to become more and more difficult for children who try to follow Christ's example. Different people have written to me about the experiences of their children:

> The worst pressure which happened this term was from our son's peer group. A 'friend' turned against him and challenged him to fight. When he refused he was dubbed 'gay' and shunned by most of his year. This caused him so much hurt that again the lower school head became involved.

In spite of opposition some who fly the flag bravely do manage to cope:

It was Tolu's first week away from home, and he seemed to have heard more cursing and swearing than in all his twelve years put together. His shocked protest met with incredulity. Apparently he was the first boy some of his classmates had ever met who did not swear. In his own inexperienced way Tolu is trying to maintain a witness, and thank God, he seems to be holding his own in every way.

Meeting opposition when young may even strengthen rather than stunt spiritual growth.

Our eldest is now a lovely balanced Christian, but she suffered considerably at school. At nine or ten, when reading her Bible at night, she would be taunted and called 'little saint'. In her teens, also at boarding school, it was the staff who exerted pressure, forbidding pre-breakfast Bible reading with friends, and disapproving strongly of the Christian meetings she led (there was no CU). She was dubbed The White Witch by some girls. Nevertheless, the group she started numbered thirty when she left, many of them whom still stand as Christians today.

Our son suffered the 'normal' amount of teasing for reading his Bible . . . our youngest daughter is too young for other pressures to be relevant, apart from swearing and taking God's name in vain, which happens all the time at school.

The problem of bad language can be encountered in any school:

You must remember that they go to a Church of England school which has strong evangelical influence from the Christian Headmaster right down to many committed Christians on the staff and a good Christian Union. The two biggest problems that they see are the swearing and the dirty jokes. When people swear, Ruth does not say anything. She reasons that they do not know God, so how can she expect her standards to be theirs. Mary says that if her friends say 'Oh God' – 'I look at them in a funny way or I clear my throat and they say "Oh, sorry, sorry!" Also when I was goofing around Nicky said to me, "Oh, piss off!" I said to her, "Don't swear." Now

53

she says, "Oh, wee off" or "Go spend a penny. I'm not swearing now." The other thing is whether to laugh or not when a dirty joke is said . . .'

Having just come from Africa, Mary found no shame in letting her friends know she was a Christian or sharing freely to that end in classroom discussion . . . When both of her best friends were here to spend the night, in our time of family devotions Mary prayed for both Sally and Kellie that they might become Christians, as they sat there on each side of her.

These experiences do suggest that where their peers are concerned we can encourage our children to take a bold stand, but with staff they are in a different position.

Target for extremists

They may feel very threatened when their beliefs are challenged by teachers in specific areas discussed in the next chapter, and ill at ease with the 'hidden curriculum', that is, the values integral to our school system which derive from Renaissance humanism. Although such values have been permeated by Christian influence they also owe much to pagan culture and thought.

Equally hostile to Christianity are many socio-political ideas entrenched in today's classroom approach, colouring the teaching of social science, history, peace studies, the arts and many other subjects. The example was raised in the House of Lords recently of teaching material which implied a similarity between our policing methods and the Nazis. Schools have become targets for a broad spectrum of political strategists: leftwingers and rightwingers, National Front and Marxists, Gay Liberation, libertarians and feminists. The Little Red School Book was circulated widely, often accompanied by subversive leaflets.

For the first time in history schoolchildren are virtually forced to take political positions, and their emotions may be torn to pieces by this premature burden. Their feelings are whipped up by malcontents and fanatics over issues which should not yet be their concern, at the expense of family life and academic progress, which should be. They are made to feel that it is actually a duty to throw stones at police, march on embassies, disrupt public order and attack the system.

There are of course schools which are completely free from political pressures, but this is a politically conscious age and it is possible that any or indeed all of these extremists may be homing in on your child's school. Parents need to be on the alert for tensions or anxiety caused by harassment, possibly from a teacher, often from politically minded older pupils, or even from activists waiting at the gates with literature. Such problems should be brought to the Head's notice; most of them prefer their schools to be used for purely educational purposes – not as recruiting grounds.

Only superstition . . .

Lucky mascots are only childish superstition, but they do indicate an attitude of misplaced faith which can be bracketed with the whole 'good luck' syndrome encompassing raffles, sweepstakes, bingo, together with omens and horoscopes, chain letters and charms. Sometimes these can make awkward situations:

When Jesus Christ really comes to live in a person, so that they are a Christian on the inside and not only on the outside, this is going to make a difference in their attitude to all sorts of things . . . one that comes up quite often is the matter of fund-raising. Raffle tickets are often given indiscriminately to every child in the class, and it can be very embarrassing for a child who knows that his parents do not approve of that method of fund raising. At the end of the day a bunch of tickets is handed in, whereas everybody else is handing in just counterfoils and a whole mass of money. But this is one of the cases where for many Christians they have to take a stand,

55

and children have to be taught that this is one of the places where their real Christian faith is going to take effect.

Maybe a parent could ease the situation by making a personal contribution to the cause. More difficult to handle are Hallowe'en celebrations when the whole school goes overboard. In one school the entire staff dressed up as witches and my students reported that some of the six-year-olds were terrified. It does seem that in some schools Hallowe'en is given greater weight than some of the Christian festivals, and this has caused anxiety to parents:

> Our daughter has been caused to make witches and read witch-orientated books, and of course children's television is now full of witches, spells, even hypnotism, so the occult is much more aggressive . . .
>
> A second area has been that of Hallowe'en activities. Not only were the children encouraged by school to view this as a similar sort of celebration as presents at Christmas, eggs at Easter, but there was pressure for peer groups to go out in the dark to play 'trick or treat' etc.

Children may find it hard to resist the pressure of friends urging them to join in 'trick or treat' pranks; but even if Hallowe'en had no occult overtones it hardly seems good character training to go around demanding treats from neighbours!

The Association of Christian Teachers has produced a useful broadsheet giving cogent reasons for repudiating Hallowe'en as an education exercise. By presenting witches and witchcraft as harmless fun, it disturbs the polarisation of evil and good in children's minds. It is a negative stroke in moral education. It fails to warn them of the very real dangers of involvement in witchcraft or any sort of occult practice.

> Occultism, witchcraft and satanism are popular and powerful fads, if nothing more. They are associated with sexual immorality, drugs, racism, sadism and even murder. Hallowe'en can

be an apparently harmless introduction to something very nasty below the surface of society (ACT pamphlet).

The broadsheet advises parents whose children attend schools that celebrate Hallowe'en to voice their concern, for it is usually introduced without much thought about what it really means. It is best to steer children clear of anything that might arouse interest in the current occult craze.

Far more sinister are the activities they may encounter at school and in friends' homes, even Christian ones; for not all Christians are aware of the real nature of the popular fantasy games on the market, such as Dungeons and Dragons, crystal balls, Osiris and tarot cards. They are all very fascinating, but also very dangerous spiritually, and when people become involved in them they can find it extremely hard to leave them alone.

Academic pressure

Under the old educational system a child was under pressure to pass the 11-plus hurdle, but whether he achieved a grammar school place or not, once within his allotted school he still found himself in a very competitive system with streaming and internal examinations. Now most authorities have introduced comprehensive education, often exams are replaced by coursework, aiming at a more relaxed system, while new types of examination have been devised to try and give each child a chance to show his best. But it is not only examinations that reveal to a child his place in relation to his peers. He knows. Competition is still largely the order of the day, and indeed must be since universities and employers need to know also.

The issue is not a simple one, for one child's pressure is another child's spur. There are children who never achieve their full potential unless an examination is hanging over their heads. Nonetheless it is encouraging that throughout the teaching profession there is a greater awareness of the distress undue pressure can cause. Research into dyslexia should now relieve many children of the charge of laziness or stupidity, and informed help enable them to avoid the pressures of illiteracy in a literate society. There is greater concern for the slow learner, the handicapped child and the linguistically, socially or parentally deprived one. This must come closer to the Christian view of each child's unique value.

School's eye view

The Headmistress of a comprehensive with an impressive record both for 'high-flyers' and also for bringing out each child's individual best, listed the school pressures she had met many times, causing behaviour problems and under-achievement.

1 A child may be forced to stay on at school against his will simply because the parent did not have the chance to do so.

2 Alternatively a child may be forced to leave against his will because the parents' attitude is 'I left school at 14, so why shouldn't he?'

3 Children are in danger of being pushed into unsuitable professions because the parent says 'I always wanted to be a doctor when I was young.'

4 Parents can expect all members of the family to be equally bright and make a less able child feel very inadequate, and thus destroy confidence.

5 There is a tendency for inexperienced staff to make this mistake too!

6 One able child in a family of less able ones can also be made to feel odd and different.

7 Some girls are made to shoulder far too much responsibility in the home – coping with babies, shopping – because mother is working. This leads to tiredness and inability to cope with school work.

8 Divided loyalties can cause problems for children selected to play in Saturday matches when they have a Saturday

job. Also applies in the evenings. Despite the strict rules concerning juvenile employment, these are frequently ignored by parents and employers.

9 Any domestic friction between parents causes problems. The child is frequently pressed to 'take sides', and this is very distressing if he loves them both equally well.

10 The arrival of a grandparent who is to share the child's room causes great resentment, especially when he is old enough to appreciate the privacy he is being forced to give up.

11 The pressure of TV advertising is tremendous as so much of it is directed at the teenager. This causes friction at home when parents are firm.

12 The fact that many parents are out all day means that houses are left empty. This can cause problems with truancy, drinking, etc, and the parents do not know what is going on.

13 Parents who have 'made good' frequently insist that children should take part in everything that is going – games, foreign holidays, outings – because they themselves did not have the chance to do so. Reticent children are sometimes pushed into doing things they really do not want to do.

14 In past years school uniform did prevent a great deal of friction caused when girls are constantly asking for money to buy the latest fashion. Generally uniform now seems to be a thing of the past, so I expect mothers just have to battle on or pay up!

15 The phrase 'liberty of the individual', which is bleated so frequently whenever anyone attempts to take a firm line, causes real problems for parents and teachers and all those who are trying to keep youngsters 'on the straight and narrow'. Some of the subversive student activities have caused problems. The youngsters think they know all the answers, and have to make adult decisions before they are ready for them.

These opinions are valuable, coming as they do from

someone who has spent her whole life in teaching in a pastoral role to parents and pupils. It is clear that parents and school must keep closely in touch if they are to discern the root causes of pressures that turn youngsters to truancy, under-achievement and vandalism. They must often take action together if they are to be of any real help to the children.

Parents' action

When there is already established a close link with the school it is much easier for parents to seek clarification and advice if some problem should crop up. If such an occasion arises the following guidelines quoted by permission from Family and Youth Concern, may be useful:

1 Be aware of the fact that the school has the avowed aim of catering for the needs of your child, and whether you believe them to be mistaken or not, they will undoubtedly have the intention of doing their best for him according to their lights.

2 Be informed of your parental rights, for example, the Inner London Education Authority, in connection with Muslim objections to sex education, has had to recognise the right of parents, enshrined in the 1944 Education Act, to have their children educated in accordance with their wishes, particularly in relation to cultural norms, religious beliefs and values. ILEA 'is concerned to respect the deeply held beliefs of a religious nature, and in certain circumstances to make special arrangements where those beliefs are incompatible with the school's programme.' This must apply to Christians too!

3 Ask for an appointment to see the Head Teacher of your child's school. Take someone with you and write down what is said in answer to your questions.

4 Note all the answers courteously. Do not be drawn into heated arguments. If you are dissatisfied tell the Head Teacher so and why. State clearly your beliefs and cultural

norms. You do not have to justify them. Ask what steps will be taken to see that your child is not indoctrinated with other standards and values.

5   On returning home write an account of what has happened and ask whoever accompanied you to check it. Send a copy to the Head Teacher asking him to confirm your understanding of the school's policy and the ways in which your wishes will be met.

6   If you are not satisfied ask for an appointment with the Chairman and Parent Governors of the school.

7   The last word on public education is the Director of Education for your area.

8   If you still do not have satisfaction, write to your Member of Parliament. Ask that the matter be taken up with the Secretary of State for Education and Science.

9   When all else fails bring the matter to the attention of your local papers, radio and TV. Public exposure can be very effective. You have been given legal rights. Why not use them?

Christian schools

There are now many parents who feel that the various pressures within the state system, and the influence of teachers who do not share their beliefs and values, could be so damaging that their right course is to withdraw their children from it altogether and place them in schools staffed and run entirely by Christians, with teaching based firmly on Christian principles and presuppositions. Even church schools, they feel, have become so secular that they do not offer a viable alternative. For them, the need for an education that holds to the truth of scripture in teaching, beliefs and values is paramount, even at the expense of such real advantages as modern science equipment, swimming pools and language laboratories.

Such a step must involve much heart-searching and a close scrutiny of motives. It may mean spending on private education, money that could have gone to relieve famine in the third world. It may mean denying the children a broad choice of subjects at O level. Nonetheless there is a steadily growing number of parents who believe that the movement for Christian schools, so well established in the USA and the Netherlands, is entirely justified and promotes the cause of the Christian faith throughout the world.

They denounce the double standards of our educational system, with its supposed neutrality, for the sake of which Christian teachers are warned against dogmatism. Yet it is itself dogmatic in its secular humanism. Thus, Christians may not teach that 'Christ is risen from the dead', but only that the disciples *said* that 'Christ is risen from the dead.'

> . . . the main reason why Christian schools are needed is that they can give children an understanding of life and themselves which is true, as opposed to the illusory faith in success, absorbing knowledge and educational power (*Spectrum*).

This is the only answer to the pressures of academic competition, political propaganda and false beliefs. Children would be relieved of the pressure of having to create their own identity, knowing that they are God's own handiwork.

In spite of this, there are many parents who feel that the Christian and secular views of education do not need to conflict on every issue. Often it is a matter of emphasis that makes the difference, and where there is a clash they can correct the influence at home. The Christian view that education should recognise the standing of each person before God accords with the secular assumption that all children should be given equal opportunity of self-fulfilment. The argument may continue, if all Christian parents were to opt for the alternative of Christian schools it would create a deep dichotomy within the social life of the nation that would probably result in greatly increased pressures for the Christian minority. Also, if children are to resist the pressures of the world that awaits them, they need to be prepared for it by living in a school which is a microcosm of the world. We are called to be salt in the world, they say, not in a salt cellar.

It is a decision that parents will take in the light of their child's personality, the nature of the schools available to them, and their confidence in the home support they can provide.

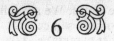

A Tree of Life

Wisdom is a tree of life to those who eat her fruit;
happy is the man who keeps on eating it.
The Lord's wisdom founded the earth;
his understanding established all the universe and space.
  King Solomon

Although the Christian religion is given formal acknowledgement in the 1944 Act, the principles underlying our educational theory rest mainly on humanist presuppositions, from which it follows that a subtle pressure towards the humanist view is inherent in the system. There are many agnostic teachers, and Christian children are likely to meet opposition or even ridicule, especially in certain subjects.

Fair balance

Science is one of the most important subjects, for it affords the basis on which a child's understanding of the universe is built. In addition to knowledge, children need to acquire the wisdom that acknowledges the spiritual dimension to the universe – only such an understanding becomes a tree of life. Yet pupils are often indoctrinated with the idea that belief in a Creator is incompatible with our present system of knowledge about the universe; that a mechanistic view is the only possible one. The serious arguments of those who find the theory of evolution incompatible with belief in God are never heard, for in the classroom it is regarded as cast-iron. A few years ago a teacher was dismissed for contending that evolution should be taught with a balanced view, allowing that there are others theories of creation. One concerned parent wrote to me:

An area which has been a source of contention since early junior school has been the subject of creation. The evolution theory is taught as fact, with no talk of an alternative idea – let alone any idea that God might have been involved! Both my children have felt unable to challenge teachers on this and felt most frustrated by the obvious bias.

Children should not have to feel threatened because of their home beliefs. It is wiser not to encourage them to cross swords with the teacher who holds all the advantages, but they may be helped to state their position simply and politely if challenged. They should be taught early that science and religion do not clash – they are answering different questions. Science is concerned with how the universe works, religion with why it exists. Science does not have all the answers; even when we fully understand DNA we shall not have disposed of God. The dialogue between science and religion is set out well in the ACT publication, *Science and Religion in the Classroom*, by Michael Poole, and in *Does God Exist? Science Says Yes*, by Alan Hayward. It is a good idea to read these and to become acquainted with new ideas and discoveries so that you can frame them up in language appropriate to your child and help him maintain a position of belief under the pressure of agnostic teaching.

Literary heritage

The English teacher is in a pivotal position in society. The teaching of English is concerned with the development of a child's whole personality, with his discovery of values and formation of attitudes. Through stories and poetry a child may gain the freedom to exercise his creative imagination; and for most people there is a direct carry-over from what they read to how they see and understand life. Literature has long been recognised as a powerful moral educator. Sir Philip Sidney saw its whole purpose as 'the winning of the soul from wickedness to virtue'.

However, the influence of reading may not be good. It depends on what is read.

Traditionally, the role of the English teacher has been to encourage and nurture a love of all the great works in our heritage, and because so much of our literature is informed by Christian values, to ensure their continuing as a formative element in our cultural identity. Many schools still follow this tradition. They choose books from the past which nonetheless have universal relevance because they give children the opportunity to think about our human freedom to choose good or evil and our purpose on this earth – books such as *Pilgrim's Progress*, *Paradise Lost*, *Adam Bede* and Shakespeare's plays. This is no longer necessarily the case. It is important that any parents looking for the right school for their child should first enquire about the English teaching, for in some schools it no longer includes works from the past which are of great value in the formation of character.

Today many teachers see life in terms of class struggle and choose books to suit their ideology, denying their pupils the classics in favour, perhaps exclusively, of twentieth century works. Often these are sordid, nihilistic and extremely depressing for the adolescent. Our children are indoctrinated accordingly, not with the unique value of the human soul, free to choose the way in a structured, moral universe created by a kindly God, but with the idea of being a cog in the social machine, purposeless, in a universe hell-bent for a nuclear holocaust. Richard Wilkins, General Secretary of the Association of Christian Teachers, has said in a letter to *Polestar*, 'English is as big a battleground for Christian parents as for teachers of religious education.'

In some schools, highly unsuitable texts are chosen for examination purposes, which does of course mean that they have to be studied in depth, not merely read and forgotten. Books chosen for reading in class, or plays chosen for drama lessons, may be equally unfortunate, containing passages with titillating descriptions of sexual experience and foul language (for example *Basketball Game*, by Julius Lester and *Come to Mecca*, by Farukh Dhondy), so that children are embarrassed by material they are given to read aloud.

All responsible teachers are concerned to offer their pupils the best, both from a literary and moral point of view, such as the Head who said, 'I am interested in academic excellence, but my first priority is the moral and spiritual growth of every child.' Nonetheless, the importance of finding out what your children are reading is illustrated in the following letter:

> Our son was uneasy about horror stories which were being read in English lessons. Having heard details, I felt we ought to make a mild protest, since the signs were that the occult could become involved. As a teacher myself, I made every effort to do this in the most correct and tactful manner. The school invited me to discuss the matter and were most sympathetic, but unfortunately the teacher concerned has continued to make our son feel awkward and abnormal by making snide remarks.

Religious education

This is an area of the curriculum where pupils who are Christians may well come under pressure when their beliefs come into conflict with a humanist or agnostic teacher. Parents, students, teachers, inspectors and local authorities are all involved in this issue, where Christians may well feel confused, even dismayed, by evident efforts to dismantle the 1944 Act, eliminating daily worship and radically altering syllabuses with a clear Christian content.

In some colleges of education the religious teaching is virtually humanism. Students are discouraged, even forbidden, from teaching Bible stories to primary age children, because children of that age find it difficult to handle abstract ideas. But God is not abstract – even though not visible, he is a person. And Bible stories are not abstract – they are a fine, concrete way of presenting ideas about God in the form of mental pictures. The story of Moses, for instance, tells the child that God will take care of him. I knew of one student who was driven to such distress by her RE tutor over this issue that she had a nervous breakdown.

During 1984 many local education authorities adopted new syllabuses, often at the initiative of RE inspectors who have generally sought to replace specifically Christian syllabuses with humanism or comparative religion. Some were closer to sociology than religion, or were concerned with subjects that could be dealt with elsewhere in the curriculum, such as drama, music, appreciation of nature and art, but made no mention of God. 'There has been a deliberate attempt to introduce humanism into the schools by the back door,' said a councillor in one such authority. 'I am a Christian and I believe I represent the vast majority of parents, who wish to see their children grow up with Christian values. I do not think that a tiny minority of agnostics should be allowed to impose their ideas on our educational system' (*Polestar*).

The objections to school worship and traditional syllabuses are mainly on the grounds that Britain is no longer a Christian country, that it is a multi-faith society, or that it is a secular society, or that Christians are likely to indoctrinate their pupils.

Agreeing to differ

In their submission to the Secretary of State concerning school worship, the Association of Christian Teachers pointed out that every child is entitled to have a spiritual component in his education and that in order to provide for this satisfactorily, provision should be made for the experience of worship. It is true that people cannot be compelled to worship, and by describing the assembly as an act of 'collective' rather than 'corporate' worship, allowance was made for those children who wished to be merely onlookers. Many pupils, parents and teachers wish worship to continue because they want the school to acknowledge the things that matter most to them. Where necessary pupils should be permitted to worship in different groups according to their religious belief or background. The ACT believed that it was neither possible nor desirable to engage in multi-faith acts of worship which blur the real differences between religions. This last point is one with which ethnic minorities generally agree.

Waving a red flag

People are generally much more worried about indoctrination by Christians than when any other belief is concerned. Yet all self-respecting RE teachers bend over backwards in order not to put pressure on their pupils in matters of belief. There is a lot of heart-searching for those who desire neither to compromise their Christian faith nor to depart from their professional position of neutrality. Yet, some feel threatened by a degree of active hostility to Christian beliefs and values in staffrooms where similar beliefs and values in minority faiths are tolerated or even admired.

Christian teachers as well as children and parents are at the mercy of syllabuses which now assume that RE is a study of man's religious quest. If this is basic to RE nowadays it goes well on the way to indoctrinating children with a belief that everyone is searching and no one has found any answers. One Oxford professor, Basil Mitchell, commented that he was very intrigued when he thought about it, that there was so much about searching in RE, yet his experience of Christianity was that we had *found* something. The 'long search syndrome' is a sort of indoctrination in that it dampens down anyone's certainty that there ever could be any revealed answers. Christians are warned about a 'missionary approach' in the classroom, but double standards are apparent in that this is actually encouraged when we are talking about other issues such as racism or sexism. It seems that any position can be tolerated, any degree of uncertainty, except the position that certainty is possible in the matter of belief. One primary school Head was even criticised by a member of the inspectorate for mentioning God in an assembly, on the grounds that this was introducing 'a controversial element'. Yet the bias and pressure *not* to believe, to which children can be subjected, needs to be realised, and corrected.

> Ann is a social worker who looks after teenagers who are in care or on probation. She has been very upset by some experiences of her elder son in a school with which she is otherwise satisfied. Religious Education, she feels, should be laying those moral and spiritual foundations whose lack underlies the wrecked lives of so many of the teenagers with whom she has to deal. But her thirteen-year-old son was taught RE by an agnostic who took advantage of his position to try to undermine his pupils' faith. Early in the year he said, 'Hands up all those who believe in God.' When a fair number put their hands up, he told them, 'I'm going to show you that there is no logical foundation for such a belief.' From time to time he asked the same question, pouring scorn on those who persisted. By the end of the year there were only three pupils still willing to raise their hands (*Polestar*).

Parents who are worried about the sort of religious education their children are receiving do have the right under the 1944 Act to withdraw them. Other undesirable pressures, such as the exposure of children to invidious material through clubs and societies, must be dealt with differently. Probably the most effective way to bring about changes is by becoming involved in the whole life of the school through the Parent-Teacher Association if there is one. We should also give all possible support to Christian teachers we may know, for they too may be feeling the pressure.

Sex education

The two areas of curriculum which deal most directly with life issues – religious education and sex education – are treated differently by the system. Parents may withdraw their children from religious education, but not from sex education. They have no control over the curriculum, so that when sex education is introduced it automatically becomes compulsory. Most parents do feel that some form of sex education is desirable. But as it is at present – promoted with a missionary zeal denied to Christians in RE, by those with vested interests in the manufacture of sex education material and contraceptives – it gives no moral guidelines; it debases the creative act which should be the expression of the deepest human love, and drives children into early, promiscuous sexual relationships which they are often unable to handle. There is an explosion of commercialisation in the schools today, happening in the name of education. In 1972 the Royal College of Obstetricians and Gynaecologists warned

> that wrongly orientated sex education could be having a result which is the exact opposite of what it was desired to achieve, in that it was arousing curiosity and the desire to experiment. The rapidly rising incidence of unplanned pregnancies in the young age group gives some support to this idea (*Unplanned pregnancy*).

Children find it hard to resist experimenting under the pressure of some sex education because they are at an age when sexual curiosity is strong, and they are too young and inexperienced to realise what may be the result. Furthermore it is taught by people in authority whose ideas the pupils will be prepared to accept because they are used to doing so.

Persuasive propaganda

Since the introduction of sex education there has been a rise in abortions to unmarried teenage girls, and an increase in venereal disease, cervical cancer and prostitution among the young. These are statistics, but the trauma of the after effects of abortion, the emotional damage of sexual relationships without love, and the nervous complaints such as anorexia nervosa, are harder to quantify.

Sex education in schools is reinforced by the influence of dedicated sex education lobbyists who promote the idea that it is acceptable for children of any age to 'have sex' of any variety, provided that no pregnancy follows. The 'sex experts' who compose and recommend sex education materials, and give advice in teenage magazines and write books, set a trend in teenage culture, which all must follow as the norm. They say that there are no rights or wrongs, provided contraceptives are used and that if that fails, there is an abortion.

The content of the subject

The content of sex education is wide-ranging. It includes not only factual detail about the biological aspects of human intercourse and reproduction, together with information about contraception, but also varied aspects of human relationships, homosexuality, love and marriage, divorce, adultery and abortion. There is nothing in this content itself to cause anxiety, but it is obvious that here again is an area of the curriculum in which the philosophy of the teacher will make a significant difference to the way in which it is approached.

A recent letter to Valerie Riches at Family and Youth Concern pinpoints a typical problem parents face. In this case a visiting family planning doctor told a group of schoolgirls that there was no need to worry about herpes and VD.

> They were not important. One girl asked whether she should come to the family planning clinic with her boy friend and was told 'That would be ideal.' A selection of rubber goods was handed round by the assistants . . . At no stage were the dangers of promiscuity touched upon.

The parent complained to the Headmistress and asked for an alternative view to be put to the girls. She received a sympathetic reply but was told that all parents had been asked beforehand if they wished their girls to attend. This parent commented: 'How many parents are afraid to say that their daughters may not go in case they are victimised and teased unmercifully?'

Since sex education is treated as a class subject it is taught in groups according to their chronological age. Children, however, do not all develop emotionally at the same rate and sometimes they are too young or too sensitive for mass teaching about something which instinct dictates is a very private affair. On this matter the DES has stated that, 'the privacy and reticence of boys and girls should be respected by all teachers, and that teachers should never in any circumstances lift the veil from their own private lives.'

The integrity of the teachers is not in question here, nor would I wish in any way to underestimate their understanding of the pupils in their care. However, on the grounds of objectivity, sex education generally is given without moral guidelines, and in this particular subject the fact that a moral dimension is missing does not make it neutral as teaching, but libertarian.

> Because of growing concern by professional people and politicians about the nature and effects of sex education, the law now decrees that parents have a right to know what is to be taught to their children about sexual behaviour. It is important that parents use this right with confidence. They should enquire carefully into courses and the material to be used under such apparently innuocuous titles as Education in Personal Relationships, Education for Family Life/Parenthood, and Health Education (Family and Youth Concern).

The teaching material itself is often dubious:

> A contraception teaching pack for use with children in schools includes puzzles and quizzes on sex and contraceptives under the heading 'Safe Sex'. Some of the illustrations have been publicly described as pornographic. Questions are asked in

one of the quizzes requiring children to give in their replies the names of brands of contraceptives. Protests by MPs led to the removal of two of the more objectionable items from the pack (*No Entry for Parents*, Family and Youth Concern).

Amongst all this propaganda for easy sex, little is said about its dangers. Young people are not warned about the high failure rate of contraception among adolescents; of the increased danger of cervical cancer to young girls, about the possibility of various venereal diseases and chronic herpes genitalia. The side effects of the Pill range from minor disorders such as headaches, weight gain and irritability to rare but serious troubles such as liver tumours, blood clots and high blood pressure. Moreover there are emotional aspects such as hormonal and personality changes, suicidal depression and inability to concentrate, leading to under-achievement at school and lost careers. In 1981 Professor Thomas Szaz, child psychiatrist, said:

> . . . sex education, as presently practised, is a mass of misinformation, misrepresentation and downright fraud. The term 'sex education' conceals far more than it reveals. . . . The upshot is that many thoughtful and well-meaning people now endorse sex education (especially in schools) as a good thing. They should, instead, oppose it as one of the most deplorable consequences of the combination of 'liberal' policies with medicalised morals.

One anxious parent wrote:

> I work as a midwife and family planning nurse and I am always seeing the disastrous results of casual sex. For this reason I am very concerned about the nature of sex education increasingly given in schools . . .
>
> My daughter reported a talk from her school Matron: 'She said we must not have sex except in a loving relationship'. I asked my daughter if she thought that was right. She said no, it was for marriage. I told her to keep that fact firmly in her head no matter what anyone else said. I rang the school

and said that an eleven-year-old could make anything of the expression 'a loving relationship'. If they couldn't teach that sex was for marriage would they please not do the subject at all. I was told again that Matron was a very moral lady and would never have said that.

Worse was to come. One day my twelve-year-old came to me tearfully. 'There's something I must ask you. What do they do with all the little babies that are aborted?' This time the children (boys and girls) had been given a lesson on abortion and contraception by the biology teacher. This had been billed for the fourth year and we certainly had not been warned of it before. The class was shown all the different contraceptives, pills, IUCDs, caps, sheaths, creams and so on. My daughter was revolted by all of it. She informed me that when she was married, she and her husband would have separate bedrooms. No doubt you will laugh as I did, but it isn't really funny! I have known some children put off for life by insensitive sex education and this is just as bad as the other danger – causing them to be promiscuous . . .

My children's experience of sex education, so far, is not as bad as that encountered by some of my friends. Their children have been shown thoroughly amoral films and some of the books available are unbelievably horrific. Parents simply *must* know what is going on, otherwise how can we look after our children? We are, after all, expected to be responsible in law for their welfare and to pick up the pieces when they go wrong.

This letter was addressed to Valerie Riches of Family and Youth Concern, which exists to promote the well-being of the family and to protect the rights of parents. They point out that:

1 In 1981 the DES published guidelines on the school curriculum which state that 'the fullest consultation and co-operation with parents are necessary before it (that is, sex education) is embarked upon. In this area, offence can be given if a school is not aware of, and sensitive to, the

cultural background of every child. Sex education is not a simple matter and is linked with attitudes and behaviour.'

2 Following a request by the Muslims that their children could be withdrawn and given alternative work ILEA has had to recognise the rights of parents enshrined in the 1944 Act to have their children educated in accordance with their wishes, particularly in relation to cultural norms, religious beliefs and moral values.

3 Ultimate parental responsibility must be accepted and respected by every school in matters of sex education/instruction.

There is a correct procedure to follow where the sex education causes concern, outlined on page 60. Family and Youth Concern are always glad to hear from parents who need advice or support or who have some relevant information to share. They have recently produced the video, *Let's Talk About Love*, suitable for use with thirteen to sixteen-year-olds, the aim of which is to counter libertarian pressure. It uses a simple story about two schoolgirls with different attitudes to allowing their boyfriends to 'go all the way'. It could be used equally in church youth fellowships or in schools – maybe in your child's sex education programme by request.

Parents can best help their children to cope with the pressure of sex education by pre-empting it; becoming themselves involved by teaching sexuality within the home: as a God-given gift which enriches the whole of personality. In preparing them to be partners in marriage in this way, parents draw close to their children and keep their confidence. The children will be less likely then to fall victims to these powerful pressures which bear on them from school and through the media and from their friends.

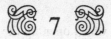 7

Pied Pipers

If young toughs tell you, 'Come and join us' – turn your back on them.
  King Solomon

'The world which confronts all of us today is morally shapeless,' said the Archbishop of Canterbury, giving the Hockerill Foundation Lecture in London. 'The old sources of moral authority seem to have dried up. The traditional equation – age plus experience plus knowledge equals authority – fails to convince any more. Certainly adulthood by itself no longer confers automatic moral authority.'

He attributed this in part to young people's having turned away from the values of the older generation. 'Can we be surprised if they turn to us and say, "This is the world which you have made with your values. What's so great about it?" ' Instead they have created their own absorbing and satisfying culture.

The absorbing culture of the teenager

Teenagers have found a corporate entity and a self-conscious awareness of being in a class of their own: neither child nor adult. A cult music and a literature have grown up to serve the needs of the adolescent – his particular problems and preoccupations. Adolescence is naturally a time of upheaval, and the insecurity of the age is further increased by the feeling that there is no solid adult back-up. Many of the problems of the young can be laid at the door of the older generation, for the lack of real authority in their lives leaves them wide open to the pressures of the peer group.

Need to identify

The characteristics which open up the way to peer-group pressure are present even in the very young. Junior school children who have recently left the tolerant and kindly ethos of their infant classroom are very sensitive to ridicule, easily embarrassed and hurt by any form of rejection by their friends. They have a great need to identify with their own age group, often one or two pals in particular, and to feel accepted by a social clique or gang.

'Jeremy is my best friend,' insisted seven-year-old Wayne, not once but many times as he accompanied his parents to buy a new bunk bed, which he was determined should be the exact replica of Jeremy's. And although his mother objects to the fact that wearing trainers day in day out makes his feet smell, he simply refuses to wear his good leather walking shoes because all the other children in the class wear trainers only.

There is the problem of the school discos. These are fund-raising events for the whole school, seven-year-olds included. Parents accompany their children, and bring their own drinks. Julie's mother does not like this. She can visualise her small daughter having to dance with some parent who smells of beer and maybe has had too much to drink. But if Julie does not go to the discos she will soon be thought snobbish or odd, and that could cause real distress. It might even cause personality problems in a sensitive child.

Children seem to quarrel and make-up with such frequency that it is easy for us to undervalue the importance of their peer-group relationships. The experiences of our own childhood have grown hazy. 'And so it comes', wrote George Eliot, 'that we can look on at the pain of our children with smiling disbelief in the reality of their pain,' and she gives as an example the misery of a boy whose mother will not let him have a coat like all the other boys. It is not the coat that bothers him but the loss of status among his peers: 'every other boy had gone into "tails" already'. 'We should not pooh-pooh the griefs of our children,' George Eliot concluded, anticipating the advice of a respected writer on family life, James Dobson. In his book, *Preparing for Adolescence*, he encourages parents to prepare their children to resist this sort of peer pressure by working hard at building their self-confidence. 'An individual with this sort of confidence often becomes a leader,' he writes. We need to take seriously the difficulties that our children will be faced with in adolescence before they reach that stage, and help them to establish a clear sense of identity so that they may become leaders themselves, and not slavishly follow the crowd.

'You don't have to be like Jeremy,' says Wayne's father. 'Have your own sort of bed. Think up your own ideas. Don't just copy someone else.' He knows that following the craze for collecting Star Wars characters has come the A-Team mania. Next Wayne will have to have a bike like his friends – and then it's only a few years before it will be the latest make of motor-bike. In a few years Julie's friends will be asking her along to teenage discos and she will have to have sufficient self-respect to resist the heavy petting that may follow.

Trouble makers

Adolescents are particularly vulnerable to peer-group pressure because they are so unsure of themselves. These are years when teenagers are ready to worry about their personal appearance and become extremely sensitive to other people's opinions. They are years when the stress of unnerving physical changes interacts with heightened emotional susceptibility, when moods swing from one extreme to another. A snub can change the teenager from elation to despair, or a smile from the right person can have him walking on air. They are years full of contradictions, for the excitement and challenge of growing up are crossed with anxieties about leaving the warm secure world of childhood.

The adolescent craves status and needs to feel independent. He may cover the walls of his room with huge
posters and cut-outs of sports and TV personalities who
are the current idols, with rock music blaring out of a
transistor and a notice on the door saying 'Keep out. This
means you.' Or he may move out into rooms shared with
someone of his own age. Yet still the need for parental
support may be there. This ambivalence may be keenest
where there are ties with a good home; it is among middle
class adolescents that the rise in juvenile delinquency has
been most dramatic.

The backing of Christian parents is invaluable, for
although it does not provide a cast-iron guarantee against
the crises of teenage rebellion, it may well be in response
to their influence and prayers that a wayward son or
daughter will eventually reach stability and wholeness.

Joanne was in a girls' Bible class which I used to lead. She
had attended Sunday School for as long as I could remember
and came from a Christian home. When she was in her early
teens she went forward at an evangelistic meeting, and we
were all thrilled to see her new enthusiasm for the Lord!
However, on leaving home she soon became open to a number
of temptations and influences she hadn't even realised existed
until then. Her enthusiasm for God cooled considerably, and
she found an exciting new world. She worked as a 'bunny-
girl' at Mayfair's Playboy Club, and later spent a summer
hostessing on private yachts, sailing round the Med. It spelt
heartache for those of us who had watched her grow up,
especially for mum and dad. But we were reminded of the
prodigal son's father in Luke 15, who let his son go – and we
held on in prayer. Eventually – like that boy – Joanne 'came
to an end of herself' and found her way back to her Saviour
(Mary Reid in *Family*).

The highly intelligent and thoughtful adolescent is as
likely to become delinquent as the less able. He is likely
to reflect on the world that is portrayed in the media and
be dismayed by what he sees. He does not enjoy the

prospect of being burnt to a cinder in a nuclear holocaust, and his heart is torn – for at this age he is extremely sensitive to the suffering of others – by the poverty and distress of the third world. Yet he is powerless to effect any change in the 'system'. He has no vote, no voice, is still denied many adult opportunities and is perhaps still restricted to the world of school. Frustration may make it appear that the only way of expressing power over others is by damaging their property through vandalism, grafitti or even arson.

Unemployment may be another factor, combining with rising world tensions to induce feelings of alienation and hopelessness which cause some to lash out at a society that appears to be cynically hard.

It may be sheer boredom that motivates the young offender who has time on his hands, a good deal of freedom, little supervision and no responsibility. Because of their immaturity and unsettled emotional state many adolescents find it hard to keep strong feelings such as anger or fear under control. Sometimes the presence and support of friends gives an increased incentive to give way to those feelings. Moreover, all those 'friends' will gang up on the one unfortunate who holds back from some lawless act or hooliganism. The trouble at and after football matches often starts in this way.

Delinquency and violence may spring from adolescent feelings of self-doubt and inferiority. A boy who thinks he is worthless may decide that defying the law is a way of getting back at society and proving his worth.

An actress speaking on the radio told how low self-esteem had affected her at the age of fifteen and she had dyed her hair as a rebellious statement: 'The chip on my shoulder was because I wasn't as bright as I'd like to have been, and I wasn't as social as I'd like to have been. I wanted people to love me, but when I opened my mouth hateful things came out.' She had adopted the punk move-ment because of her hatred of school and her hatred of her childhood, and because she wanted to rebel against everything.

Stuck on glue

Speaking to a group of nurses, a Scotland Yard detective referred to glue-sniffing as 'kid's stuff'. Children sometimes try it as a way of getting accepted by the gang, and later the majority will drop it for some other activity which offers the same attraction of parental disapproval and peer challenge. However, some do become addicted and there may be tragic consequences. Some may die as a direct result of inhaling fumes, especially if an aerosol is used, and many have died from side-effects such as choking on vomit or walking into traffic or falling down embankments or out of windows, having lost all sense of danger. Some have put their heads in bags in order to inhale, and have died from asphyxiation while in an inebriated state.

All sorts of solvents, as well as glue, are used, such as nail varnish remover, hairspray, cleaning agents, deodorants, which can have long-term poisonous effects, causing damage to the central nervous system, the brain, heart, liver and kidneys. Children will make sniffing a group activity, but those most in danger are the ones who do it on their own. They may hide the solvent in crisps bags or dab it on ties or tissues and carry on right under the noses of adults. A schoolgirl said:

> There's a girl in my English class at school who sniffs thinner and glue during the lesson without being seen. She puts it on a tissue, sniffs it and then goes off to the toilets. She also supplies a crumbly powder, which is a drug called 'speed' and girls come up to her and ask for it.

Children are most at risk during the years between eight and eighteen, and not only those from a deprived background. Seventy per cent of the pupils at an expensive public school were found to be sniffing. Apart from the more obvious symptoms such as an eczema rash and an appearance of drunkenness, a fall in academic performance, increased aggression and delinquency may all be pointers to this insidious habit. The most likely children to be at risk are those from broken homes or homes where there is little affection so that the companionship of other sniffers is particularly attractive:

> I used to be a glue sniffer. The first time I tried sniffing I was eleven years old, and I was with some of my mates in an old house. I quite liked it, but I didn't do it again for some time, not until I had to go into a children's home. I was put there because I wouldn't go to school. I soon started to sniff again. There were some garages opposite the home and I went over and saw other youngsters sniffing, so I joined in . . . I started to sniff every week, under some garages where lots of kids went sniffing. My sniffing got worse, until I was sniffing every day and sometimes twice a day . . . I was addicted to glue and I couldn't stop. I got suspended from school, which meant I was sniffing all day as well as all night . . . all I wanted to do was sniff (National Campaign Against Solvent Abuse).

Parents or teachers who have noticed the symptoms mentioned or have other reasons to suspect a child has become involved should try to discuss the problem in a free and relaxed manner, Family relationships may be at the root of it, or pressures from other causes. The help of a doctor may be imperative; and it may be wise to tell the police so that they can visit the homes of the other children and warn parents of the danger. The foster father of the boy just quoted called on the assistance of the NCASA:

> My best friend said he would try and help me stop, and so did NCASA. The sores I had around my mouth have gone now, and I feel great. But while I was coming off I was bad. I felt sick. I had pains in my chest and I thought I was dying. After a couple of weeks that feeling goes away and now I'm a different person. My advice to others who are thinking of trying it is: DON'T.

Another little drink

We used to think of alcohol as being a parents' problem, but it is becoming increasingly the problem of the children themselves. Drink is more available now because it is more popular in the home. Television and advertising, which have had to draw back where smoking is concerned, still churn out the image of the sophisticated drinker. A speaker on the radio, giving a warning about under-age alcoholism, mentioned that there are many eleven-year-olds for whom a glass of vodka a day was not uncommon.

To be an alcoholic is to have a potentially fatal disease. No one can tell who is a potential alcoholic, nor at what age the habit may take hold. The question of drinking is one of the many on which Christians hold different views. Some parents give their children an example of teetotalism and have no alcohol in the house. Others feel that an understanding of moderation will give their children a better hope of resisting peer pressure to drink to excess.

For their own protection, adolescents should be put in full possession of the facts about alcoholism and the danger of uncontrolled drinking. *Alateen* is an organisation which aims to do this and also to support those families which have been broken by drink. Children may be subject to pressures connected with drink not only from their peers urging them to excess, but also from parents who are addictive drinkers:

My mum died when I was fifteen and I went to live with my uncle, aunt and cousin. My uncle seemed to take over from my parents and I became very close to him. But he was drinking and that made his personality change . . .
I denied anything was wrong with my uncle and wouldn't let any of my friends see him. I was frightened of what they would think and how it would reflect back on me. I was afraid of being the laughing stock at school. I was very lonely . . .
My friends didn't know anything was wrong . . . I became

withdrawn . . . eventually I was questioning my sanity. I even began to blame God.

I went along to *Alateen* and there I began to understand about alcoholism being a disease. I had blamed my uncle for hurting me emotionally, spiritually and physically, but I now see it was the perfect excuse for everything that went wrong, for avoiding the truth about myself and my own life. It was like blaming someone for having cancer . . . I am outgoing now. I have a new attitude that enables me to enjoy life (Band of Hope).

Facing the Dragon

The greatest menace for today's youngsters is the drug scene. A challenge to experiment with smoking pot at a teenage party has resulted in the destruction of many a budding personality; the popping of pills in the playground has eventually brought an end to many a young life. It is not confined to pop stars nor to the derelicts of society, but is a very real danger to the children of good homes.

> I come from a strong and loving family and the first eighteen years of my life were spent at good schools and in a secure, happy and drug-free environment. When I began using heroin my life had already been won over by drugs; they were my god and I would do nothing without them. I first used heroin to make me feel good, then to improve an evening out, and finally, in order to get out of bed and face the day so I could get some more. I was hooked from that first time (Band of Hope).

It is like a cancer working its way through the system. Youngsters who have become enslaved by pushers will in turn put pressure on their friends to buy the less addictive drugs from them, in order to finance their craving.

Drugs are particularly attractive to those who feel unable to cope with life, with the stresses and strains of growing up, and to those who have a low opinion of their worth. Many of the victims are also those who have succumbed to despair in the current hysteria about nuclear war. Campaigners for peace, however well-intentioned, must take some of the responsibility for inducing a state of panic fear among the young. The Bible does not spell out the way this world will end; but it does clearly promise that Christ will come again and that he will take those who are his to be with him. What more can we ask? We all have to die some way. We may never have to face a nuclear holocaust, but the presence of lethal drugs among our young is something we do have to face here and now.

Many adolescents go through a period of deep pessimism. They are politically and personally sensitive and fear what the future may hold for the world and for themselves. They need the inner assurance that the future is under the control of Christ, not of men – that 'behind the dim unknown stands God, keeping watch above his own.' They also need parents in whom they can confide their fears and who give them an example of faith, and the belief that even though we all experience times of sorrow and disappointment, life is fundamentally good. They need opportunities for making friends with creative interests and plenty of activities that provide outlets for their abilities, so that they gain a sense of fulfilment and personal worth.

In an interview by the *Journal of School Health*, Mrs Nancy Reagan said that 'the reason she was never tempted by drugs was that she liked herself just as she was and didn't want to do anything that might change that. Self-respect and self-esteem are very important and can't be learned too early, because they become a child's shield and armour.'

Where to get help

There are some very helpful leaflets available for professionals, parents and children from the DHSS. 'What *every parent* should know about drugs' gives basic facts on drugs and drug-taking; 'What parents can do about drugs' offers information and advice to parents concerned about their teenager's health and well-being; and 'Drug misuse: a basic briefing' is a factual guide for professionals and parents. The Life-Anew Trust at Cloud House exists to help young people who have become invlved with heroin. Among the first symptoms of drug abuse is a withdrawal of confidence, a growing secrecy and gradual personality change. Parents who have such cause for anxiety would do well to phone Cloud House or one of the other organisations listed under 'Helpful Addresses'.

Before I entered treatment my family had chosen, through love, to abandon me. I did not care whether I lived or died. It was only at this point that I knew I had to do something about my problem so I phoned Cloud House and within three hours I was walking through the doors . . . I sat down, terrified, but I felt I was with people who understood. Since that day I have not looked back. Only in astonishment. I chose to go one hundred per cent for recovery and am still in process of doing that. Life has taken on a new meaning (Life Anew).

Before things get to this stage it is important to work at keeping the lines of communication open as the children grow into adolescence. It may well be true that young people who have good relationships with their parents are less likely to feel the need to try drugs:

No use ignoring your children for years, treating them as rubbish and their dreams as stupid – and then suddenly expect them to take your opinions seriously. If you have shown your children throughout their lives that you are happy, they will believe you when you talk of serious matters. Conversely, if they have deduced from your example that life is not worth living is it surprising that they take a suicidal path? Show that happiness – and intense happiness – can be got in moral, legal ways: walks in the country, ballet, music, poetry, literature, church services, singing. Show that unhappiness (loss by death or because a friend then chooses someone else, failure in an examination or choice of career) can be coped with, leaving you stronger after the initial agony – instead of becoming weaker and weaker with false crutches (*Alternative Alternative*, Dave Parry).

Dating – 'Everybody's doing it.'

'You're much too young,' is quite likely to be the reaction when a boy or girl comes home excited by the prospect of a first date. Our children will in one sense always be children to us, and the first date is the first indication that they will one day be leaving the nest. However, we would not be parents if we had not gone through this ourselves, and we should look on our children's awakening to these relationships with shared pleasure, making these few precious years a happy time for the whole family – rather than pulling up the drawbridge and repelling all comers.

'But all my friends are dating,' is likely to be the reply. 'Everyone is doing it.' We have to realise, first, that this generation of children reaches puberty earlier than previous ones, and secondly, that the pressure to begin dating is very strong when all the friends are matching up in couples. We are likely to have two questions in mind. Who is the date? Is it someone we would approve? And, what do they mean by 'dating'? Is it to be a group, a foursome, or just the two of them – and where? What indeed do they mean by 'Everybody's doing it?' Doing *what*, we wonder.

Who is the date?

Our children's friends are likely to be a mixture of Christians and non-believers drawn from school and neighbourhood, church and clubs. Our great hope will be that they do not enter into a deep relationship with someone who is not a Christian, so it would be wise to advise them right from the start that they may avoid heartache by not accepting dates with non-Christians. As with all steps which will affect their future they should seek God's will with regard to their dating and relationships with the opposite sex. Remind them of the practical good sense of the biblical guideline not to be unequally yoked so that they avoid becoming involved with the wrong person. But Christians are as impetuous as all young people so this may not work. Moreover Christians are often in such a minority that your son or daughter may not have very much choice.

Where affairs of the heart are concerned it is better not to put your teenager on the spot by taking an intransigent, 'Never darken my door again' attitude if he does date without your approval. That may drive him or her the other way. Or if you have a closely bonded child you may tear their heartstrings in a conflict of loyalty.

It is good for teenagers to date – not merely with the aim of finding a partner for life – but also to learn how to handle relationships with both Christians and non-Christians, to explore all sorts of interests, to have fun, to get exercise and so on. A teenager who is not allowed to go out and date may become lonely and depressed, losing self-esteem. She may also withdraw from her parents. On the other hand boys and girls who show no desire to date should not be pushed. They are not abnormal. Either way this is an area where the confidentiality and friendship between parent and child can easily be spoilt. Advice in terms of reason or encouragement is valuable and often welcome, but interference is not.

It may be that a teenager is longing to date, but cannot find anyone who wants to go out with her. This can be a very demoralising experience, for as her opinion of herself suffers, so she is likely to become less interesting and more isolated. It is a vicious circle. She needs a great deal of family support so that she does not think 'I'm no good – nobody wants me.' The best way to help her is not to be so sympathetic that she becomes sorry for herself, but to help her to become more likeable. Without making her self-conscious help her to find clothes and hairstyles that make the most of her appearance, to get rid of those spots and to use make-up that is attractive, not flamboyant. More important, tell her that although good looks are an asset, a teenager does not have to be a striking beauty in order to be popular. More effective is it to be a good sport, fun to be with, to have a worthy self-image (for this will be reflected in the opinions of others) and respect and warm affection for friends.

Is this Mr Right?

The best hope for a stable and happy relationship is to find someone with similar tastes, interests and values before romance begins to blossom. How do we help our teenager to make the right choice? First, give them a model of what a love relationship can be. Show them that love is not simply a beautiful thing that you feel (though it certainly is that) but also a strong bond that can carry you through the hard places and survives disagreements, even quarrels. Show them unselfishness, affection and fun together. Tell them how you met and fell in love and all the tender and humorous little things that made your courtship such a wonderful time. They'll like that. I know an eight-year-old who made the long car journey from the east to the west coast pass in high spirits by demanding that his parents should tell him about how they came to love each other and to marry. Show them what is wrong with the relationships in soap operas on TV and in the novels and comics that they read. Many teenage girls read *Wuthering Heights* and *Pride and Prejudice* for the romantic interest. Help them to see where Cathy and Heathcliff came unstuck and what was needed to make Elizabeth Bennett and Darcy into perfect partners for each other.

Then, get to know their friends so that they do not hear you speak about them only when you disapprove. Invite them into your home, chat with them in a relaxed atmosphere, find their interests and discuss with them their ideas on what is wrong with the world. Then you will have grounds for any evaluation of their qualities and your teenager is more likely to listen with tolerance.

Help them to distinguish between love and infatuation. Ask them 'Would you like to have this person as the father/mother of your children?' 'Do you have the same values, standards, sense of humour?' 'Can you be happy with him/her without any thought of making love?' 'What sort of things make you quarrel, and how is the quarrel resolved?' 'Could you endure a long separation and stay in love?'

What do they mean by dating?

By dating some teenagers mean holding hands in a cinema; for others it may mean 'going all the way' on a sofa in a friend's flat.

Parents have the responsibility, no matter how good the sex education at school, of making sure that their own teenager understands all that is involved in having a sexual relationship. Ideally sex education should come from the parents but for some this subject, if not actually taboo, is still embarrassing, so we should be grateful for the factual information included in the school curriculum. As we have seen, however, it may not make clear the dangers of venereal disease and of early and promiscuous intercourse. By stressing the availability of contraceptives it may suggest that sexual activity is right and normal. Teenagers may not realise the failure rate of contraceptives or that sleeping around may damage their ability to later make a deep and permanent relationship; they do not consider that the consequences of casual sex may mean providing for a baby, or killing it in the womb. Parents need to get all this straight. They need to inject the moral and spiritual values omitted by the schools and to encourage their children to follow the Bible teaching and standards in all matters relating to the opposite sex, so that they do not give way to the pressures of the world.

The Bible is specific about fornication, adultery and homosexuality but it does not say much about kissing and petting. However, it does say a lot about truth, right conduct and human relationships. It does tell us to love one another and gives a clear picture of what love really means – kindness, goodness, self-control and faithfulness (1 Corinthians 13). We can help teenagers to avoid temptation by discouraging them from reading novels or watching films that are likely to arouse them sexually; by explaining to girls the insensitivity of wearing next-to-nothing bikinis and see-through blouses; by avoiding leaving them in compromising situations, for example, a teenage boy and girl baby-sitting alone in a house; parties where there will be drinking, flirting and couples going off alone; late night car rides, even unsupervised church activities can be unwise.

We need to be just as consistent with our teenagers as with younger children, and they should be given guidelines of behaviour so that they are in no doubt as to where we draw the line. A boy should be told when he is to bring your daughter home and the consequences of failing to do so; he should phone if they are going to be late; you must know where they are going; some places are out of bounds; he should treat her as he would like his sister to be treated. They should not be dating until you feel they are ready.

Christian teenagers should also be reminded to give the Lord prior place before all human relationships, regarding sex as his pure gift to be enjoyed fully only in marriage. We cannot lay down the law with teenagers, for that is likely to backfire. Giving them guidelines can only be in the nature of advice, and gradually they must have the freedom to make their own choices. We have to trust them to God, pray for them, and if they do make mistakes forgive them and support them still.

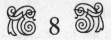

The World Around

> We know that we are children of God and that all the
> rest of the world around is under Satan's control.
> *St John*

Our children are growing up in a different world from the
one we knew as children. The nuclear family is no longer
the unquestioned framework for raising children, and this
has weakened a traditional source of stability, leaving a
feeling of rootlessness.

The rape of virgin minds

The world of our children is virtually controlled by the
media, which portrays a much more exciting world than
the real one. Everything is highly coloured, fast, slick,
more professional and sophisticated, so that family, home
and school can seem boring by contrast. On the screen,
events have results that become apparent within minutes,
while in real life cause and effect take time, a career needs
years of study and relationships develop slowly.

It is difficult to resist values presented in such compel-
ling terms. If the media approves sex outside marriage,
then it will be OK for the teenager; if the affluent lifestyle
seems glamorous or the hippie life looks fun, then he will
despise his suburban semi; if peer group solidarity spells
happiness on the screen, he will stick in with the group.
We are living through a nationwide rape of innocence.
Before they have a chance to explore real life, or to learn
insights which would enable them to discriminate, the
media assault threatens to seduce and mould our youngsters' virgin minds.

The language trap

'You must not tell lies to children', wrote Yevtushenko. One of the hazards our children face is that of believing the lies with which they are bombarded. Our first task is to make them aware that although the purpose of language is to communicate, it may not always communicate the truth. Words may equally be used to deceive. Unless they realise this they are at the mercy of anyone who wants to manipulate them, of the ambitious politician and the unscrupulous advertiser.

Language is framed to present things as they appear to the speaker, even though he means to be objective. But often his motivation is in fact disingenuous. He is selling some product or some social or political theory, or trying to change our way of life. Even news items are shaped by the speakers' prejudices to draw a certain response from the listeners. Examples of deviousness must occur to everyone. Society might view abortion differently if it had always been called 'the murder of a baby in the womb' instead of 'the termination of a pregnancy.' We do not have strikes, we have 'industrial action' – it sounds better.

Media reporting sways public opinion, tries and judges and misrepresents by what it omits as well as by what it includes, by presenting only one side of a controversial question, or by bullying tactics in interviews. Commercial advertising is equally manipulative, and much is directed specifically at children, dangling expensive toys, bicycles and electronic gimmicks before their spellbound eyes. However, such obvious sales pressure can make good material for children to learn to use their discernment skills. While watching together ask some pertinent questions: 'Do you really think using that brand of soap will make her more attractive?' We cannot protect children from all negative influences, but we can teach them to be independent thinkers, to examine the current slogans and platitudes, to study words and expressions and to realise that the media picture of life is false.

Upside down

But it is not only words that convey phoney ideas. The visual impact of the environment also assaults the child with an upside down statement about life. Status and wealth and beauty have no lasting value. When the stars fall and this vast universe crumbles, it is love that will endure and goodness that will triumph. Two things need to be said:

1 This is the world we have made or allowed to be made. As someone has said, the only thing needful for evil to flourish is for good men to do nothing. Perhaps we have done nothing for too long – except for a few lone voices such as Mary Whitehouse and Victoria Gillick. *We* are responsible for the situation our youngsters face – not they. Nonetheless they are beings with free will, and our job is to help them stay the right way up in this upside down world.
2 We must not be driven into a defensive huddle, seeing only evil in everything. We cannot isolate our children from the realities of their environment, but we can help them to sort out what is good and wholesome.

Bringing up a divergent thinker

Children who have learnt to think for themselves are not at the mercy of their environment. They can resist the pressure of the media and the peer group. In some respects teenagers are no different from little children. They all learn by imitation. The way to teach them to be selective – make right choices, to know the best from the second-rate – is to be selective yourself: buying clothes which suit you, not just the fashion; turning off the TV when it offends; voicing displeasure at blue jokes and bad language. Watching you, they learn to be themselves.

We owe our children valid reasons for our choices: why we approve, for instance, of some carefully researched documentary, or a speech that does not rely on abuse but raises clear issues into debate. Such training in discrimination should be broadly based on literary, aesthetic and rational, as well as moral grounds, avoiding a narrow, legalistic approach which might make a teenager less likely to listen seriously to what we have to say.

Take an interest in what they are reading or viewing and share some thoughtful analysis. Can you believe in the characters? Do they behave as people do in real life? Does the plot seem contrived or does it evolve naturally out of the interaction of character and event? What is the book/film saying? Would it arouse sexual feelings or a fascination with the occult? Asked if there were dangers for Christians in watching violent films, one teenager wrote, 'No, of course not. Why should they react differently? They're humans aren't they?'

Another wrote,

> 'I don't think it is right for Christians to watch such films. Violence can get into the sub-conscious and affect the person mentally. Some films make violence look attractive and funny. They lighten it so that it does not seem so bad. It is treated as a joke. Lives are counted as worthless. Some suggest that it is right to return violence with violence. I disagree with this attitude. Jesus said, 'If someone strikes you on the right cheek turn to him the other also.'

There are many television programmes which, although they have no explicit Christian content, offer basic Christian values, for example, *The Waltons*, *Barchester Towers* and other revivals of classics. They may show for instance good family relationships or honourable conduct. Even in the controversial *Grange Hill* lying and deceitfulness are made unattractive. Moral choice between loyalty to friends and seeing justice done demands a close scrutiny of Christian principle. For instance, if you know your friend has stolen the dinner money, should you tell? Or, how would Jesus relate to the lonely boy who is rejected by the class? Such examples are very important to children in their teen years for they reveal that the classroom and playground are battlegrounds on which the issues of Christian belief are tested.

Developing criteria

I believe we should offer children, even from their earliest years, the opportunity of knowing the best in art, music and literature. Young children can enjoy good music and works of art, and there are also excellent modern illustrators of children's books, such as Shirley Hughes and the Brambly Hedge artist. Instead of getting hooked on comics and fantasy magazines they should be exploring the children's classics and the work of first-rate writers such as Philippa Pearce and Rosemary Sutcliff. We should take them to art galleries, exhibitions, museums, concerts, opera and ballet. Only an acquaintance with the best will give them the critical judgement to reject the second-rate.

Teenagers do not have the perspective to see the contrast between Christ's teaching and our worldly views. In the soap operas people are valued for their wealth or good looks. What then means 'Blessed are the poor in spirit' or 'The meek shall inherit the earth'? Such questions pinpoint the spiritual implications of the programmes they watch.

Vanity fair

Childhood is disappearing. The sophisticated child takes a short cut into the adult world, taking on board all the 'in' ideas of fashion, disco dancing and behaviour. The golden age of innocence and carefree happiness is growing ever shorter. Elizabethan children were dressed as adults in their ruffs and farthingales, and Victorian children toiled in mines and factories before they were seven. During the last hundred years or so the childhood of the Western world has been a carefully protected time, but now we are turning back the clock.

97

Many children view explicit sex scenes before they are able to cope emotionally and a high proportion have seen pornographic or violent video films. A four-year-old girl had watched a rape scene on video and she prattled about it in nursery school the next day. When questioned about this by her horrified teacher, the child's mother replied with a laugh, 'Well, she's got to learn about sex some time!' No one can tell what effect this experience may have on her relationship with men when she grows up.

Advertising also propels children prematurely into the adult world with products designed for them such as lipstick, nail polish and face cream, appropriately named to appeal to the teenies.

Note, too, the toy market. Dolls are no longer something cuddly to love, they are something sophisticated to emulate – a visual image of what the child is aiming for in growing up, a curvaceous sex object with a flamboyant wardrobe for every occasion and a Dallas-type lifestyle which includes a magnificent car and a horse of her own. No child who owns the doll is content until she owns the car and the horse – such is the cunning of the manufacturers.

The toy market has cashed in on the collecting urge of the junior. Children have always been collectors. Once it was beautiful things: feathers, wild flowers, shells: now it is dreary bits of plastic moulded into monsters or space men with a soul-destroying sameness. The carefully preserved dried grasses and leaves of the past gave children a chance to exercise aesthetic appreciation and taught them much about the natural world, and patience. Now the pressure is on to seek instant satisfaction from man-made things, not those created by God.

The fantasy game characters are expensive, even though made of cheap plastic, because advertising has created such a demand. Likewise the almost identical space soldiers must all be collected for their different flashes. My grandson lets me know from time to time which he is missing!

Brute strength

The fantasy games and star wars characters have hideously exaggerated muscles, huge shoulders, bursting chests, and so little clothing that they give a feeling of perverted sexuality. What does all this teach our children? It hammers home the glorification of sheer brute strength. It communicates the message that physical power is to be admired, sought after, identified with. It gives the impression that the man to take as your model is the one who can tie his enemy's legs in a knot and loop them around his neck.

How can we respond to these market forces? First we must recognise how heavily the pressures of advertising are thrust upon the seven-year-old who has competing friends and an inner collecting urge. To be stopped in the midst of some project is frustrating. All training is best done by positive means, and maybe we can channel this urge into some hobby which is not at the mercy of the money-makers, and where peer competition can become a group project instead, like swopping stamps or making models together.

Following fashion

Provocative bikinis may involve a moral issue, but broadly speaking fashion is simply a matter of taste. Today's freedom should prevent us from equating Christianity with neat hair and formal clothes. Yet dress does reflect the wearer, and we tend to adopt the image our clothes create. There was a 'tough guy' in one school where I taught. He used to swagger in among his cowed classmates wearing a leather jacket with a huge fur collar. One very hot day he was persuaded to take it off. There was a startling transformation as he slipped shyly into his seat. He had left the bully boy image in the leather jacket, and wearing a pale blue sweater, was just another small pupil.

Today's unisex fashions are a sort of social conditioning. Note too the witch-like overtones of trendy

99

make-up. Children are targets for the designers and it is important to encourage them to express their own personality in what they wear. 'Be yourselves,' a student health doctor encouraged the girls in an audience of school leavers off to campus life. 'Wear your pretty dresses, if that's the image natural for you. Don't be afraid of being feminine.'

Children will take on the fashions and behaviour they see on the screen. At three years old, Emily can give a convincing imitation of her hero, Boy George, while seven-year-old Jonathan can do all the finger-clicking, hip-rolling antics of the rock groups. Some parents fear that the disco dancing their children see and do may have a corrupting influence. 'It isn't just dancing,' said one mother, 'it's sexual signalling'.

Parents may have different opinions about this. Movement is the very essence of life to all young children. They are far happier running or jumping or dancing about than sitting still, and the sheer exuberance and vitality of disco dancing meets an urgent need of restless growing limbs and bodies. Whatever their position, sensible parents will keep an eye on the disco-dancing youngster for any effects or spin-offs such as habitual late nights, loss of concentration and poor school performance, diminished hearing and withdrawal of openness.

Rock and roll

Rock music is another controversial area. A survey by the British Market Research Bureau for the music trade reveals that fifteen per cent of all pop singles are bought by the eight to thirteen age group. This is surprisingly young. Moreover it is one of the factors in family life which can cause a rift in parent/child relationships. If your child is deeply into rock it is advisable to know about it yourself so you can discuss it with a basis of fact. There is no denying that it does have some possibilities of danger. One of its features is the complete dominance of the beat, sometimes taken directly from the drum beats of heathen rituals. Added to the constant driving beat is an intensity of sound which often reaches an uncontrolled wild pitch equivalent to the level at which rivetters wear ear plugs. This combination can have a mind-blowing effect, while the atmosphere of chaos, and the sensual, neurotic and even blasphemous words often used are degrading and morally destructive. Indeed the lyrics often promote sex and sexual perversion, drugs and revolution; messages which gather intensity from the incessant noise and driving beat to produce an imbalance in the brain which can destroy inhibition and normal reaction. It can induce a zombie-like state, altering the natural responses in the same way as drugs or transcendental meditation can.

The sexual implications of much rock and roll (which is a slang term for sexual intercourse) are very obvious, as are the gestures and movements of rock stars on the stage. Often the message is a homosexual one. The manager of the Rolling Stones has said, 'Rock music is sex and you have to hit teenagers in the face with it.' Similarly, Chris Stein, guitarist of Blondie said, 'Everybody takes it for granted that rock and roll is synonymous with sex.'

In spite of the sinister nature of this music, Christian rock fans maintain that Christian rock is not only different, but that it can be an instrument of worship, that it communicates with young people and can bring some of them to Christ. It is certainly true that it has an appeal for many young Christians, though whether it offers them an uplifting experience or a soul-destroying temptation is a matter of opinion. Cliff Richard and others say that music can never be wrong in itself since God created it, and there are dedicated Christians who see nothing wrong in it. They would doubtless point out that even heathen temples can be exorcised, sanctified, dedicated to God's service and indwelt by the Holy Spirit. In this country, chapels and churches stand over sites once used for pagan rites.

All these issues should be discussed openly with teenagers who are hooked on rock. They will be more ready to listen to any parental objections if they are shown to be based on an informed opinion and good sense. Teenagers will not come to their parents with their problems if they have the impression that the older generation has no understanding of those things which motivate them and move them deeply.

Fumes from the pit

Rock music is by no means the only channel which the media opens to occult influence. There has been an explosion of interest in the supernatural, stimulated by such films as *The Omen*, *The Exorcist* and *Rosemary's Baby*. Radio and TV interviews which have the force of propaganda now give a respectable image to yoga, astrologers, witches, spiritualists and various assorted gurus, but the sombre fact is that thousands of people have already become victims of this revival of interest in medieval practices and beliefs. Broken homes, twisted minds, fear, torment, oppression, suicide and premature death: any of these may result, and indeed have resulted, from dabbling in the occult, especially in such pseudo-religions as scientology, voodoo, alchemy and black magic. Teenagers are more likely to lay themselves open to the power of malignant evil by practising transcendental meditation, watching late night horror films, reading magazines and books on the supernatural or playing with games such as ouija, Osiris or Dungeons and Dragons. There is abundant evidence of demon possession resulting from experiments with such spiritually dangerous games for they open a door to the occult. Dungeons and Dragons has taken America by storm and is now widely played here, especially among schoolchildren and even by unsuspecting Christians. The advertisement reads:

The original adult fantasy role-playing game for age twelve

and up, which gives you worlds of sword and sorcery adventure and allows your imagination free rein. You create a game persona – a wizard or fighter, cleric or thief, dwarf, elf or half-ling, nearly any sort of character you desire. By defeating terrible monsters your game persona acquires mighty magical items, wealth and greater abilities to face challenging situations still to come.

One typical adventure is described in the instructions:

> There is an evil chapel, demons depicted on a tapestry, with a stone altar stained with dried blood . . . and a temple of evil chaos. As soon as the party enters the place, black candles will come alight magically, shooting forth a disgusting radiance. Shapeless forms will dance and sway . . . chanting a hymn to chaotic evil. There are also chambers of the evil priest with a demon idol.

There is a more advanced game which is even more explicitly occult. The makers claim that 'it is so mind-unleashing as to come near reality . . . This is a world where monsters, good and evil priests, fierce demons, even gods themselves may enter your character's life . . . The casting of spells, clerical and magical, is a very important aspect of play . . . The mystical symbols impressed on the brain carry power and speaking the spell discharges this power.'

The game introduces the players to the practice of magic arts including levitation, ESP and clairvoyance. In an explanatory pamphlet the Rev. A.R. Higton has written:

> Each player is aligned to a particular cause, one of which is neutral evil, which holds that 'pure evil is all in all'. Everyone chooses to become a character, for example, a cleric dedicated to one or more of the gods. He can use holy or unholy items including a cross or holy water. Once the player has chosen a character he becomes that persona for the purposes of the game.

103

The game is not a one-off thing but is played over and over again so that it can really take a hold on the players' minds – children may need help to give it up. The Devil uses its tremendous fascination to get people into his power, and the Bible gives very strong warnings against the practice of magic arts (Revelation 21.8).

Table turning, seances and all attempts to gain forbidden knowledge are equally dangerous and it is particularly important to warn youngsters who will be away from home that such activities are not harmless games. Here is Branse Burbridge's account of a fearful experience in a youth hostel:

'No! Not a seance! Don't talk about it!' He sat up in bed, rigid with fear. It was past 2 a.m. The chimes from the church clock had faded, merging into the eerie sound of a cat's wail. In the youth hostel, half the dormitory had been asleep, the rest talking intermittently. The sound of cat and clock in the dark had produced the inevitable ghost stories. Then someone suggested a seance. Then Richard's reaction. The others realised that they couldn't even get through to him. He gabbled on frantically, clawing at his face. They could scarcely believe that he could change so suddenly.

'Quick, go and get one of the staff.' They were wide awake now.

John raced upstairs and woke me and a colleague. 'We don't like the look of Richard at all. His pulse is racing. He's been shouting and trying to scratch his eyes out.'

Richard's eyes were closed, his pulse certainly was racing. The nails of his left hand dug into his palm, his body was rigid and his right hand was clamped against his face.

I said, 'I don't think a doctor can help. Richard's got into the power of an evil spirit – perhaps some time ago – and it's got him now. I know that Jesus conquered these evil powers when he died on the cross. So we've got to apply this victory now so that Richard can be free. We need to pray.'

They weren't used to praying. Some were sceptical. But all were afraid of the strangeness and saw something of the seriousness of the situation. They gathered round, while my colleague, Hugh, exerting considerable force, held Richard's hand away from his face.

'Lord God, we thank you that our Saviour Jesus Christ has defeated Satan and broken his power. We ask you therefore in the name of Jesus to send away this evil spirit from Richard. Don't let it touch him again, nor any other member of this group' (ISCF Viewpoint).

The advance of the occult via the media has become increasingly aggressive and our environment is heavy with these fumes from the pit. If you are aware that your child has been involved with fortune telling or any of these activities you must help him to break from it and turn to Jesus Christ in faith. Only Christ can give him the spiritual strength to resist the evil fascination and to experience victory in the future. In some cases it is imperative to call on the help of someone who has expert knowledge.

Fantasy fiction

Children's vulnerability makes them desirable material for Satan's offensive. Even a short visit to the children's library will reveal how far their world of imagination has been invaded by the supernatural, in the form of witches, ghosts, vampires and demon spirits. This is not all bad, however. A line-up of easily visualised characters – witches and dragons on the evil side; knights and fairies championing the good – can aid children in their task of acquiring moral definition before they are capable of manipulating moral ideas in the abstract. Traditional fairy tales have this useful function. It is obviously important though, that evil should be seen as repulsive and the reader's sympathies drawn towards the good.

In the popular game books and magazines now on the market these issues are confused and, as in the Dungeons and Dragons game, the reader may be invited to identify with evil. Most of them have medieval or science fiction type settings and draw on legend for their quest themes.

They are dominated by ideas and characters of the occult, with spells, magic potions and enchantment. These are all very fascinating to children, but it is important to check the actual content carefully for they vary widely in values, and some of them are a negative influence in moral education and a source of spiritual danger. *The Grailquest* in the Solo Fantasy Gamebook series by J.H. Brennan echoes Arthurian ideas of valour and encourages the reader to behave nobly: 'From King Arthur's court at Camelot, knights of the Table Round set forth on quests of valour – but *you* have been chosen to undertake the most perilous missions of all . . . to rescue Queen Guinevere.'

The reader is invited to show mercy: 'Don't kill him, Pip. That isn't chivalry!' we are exhorted as our opponent falls to the ground defenceless.

Unfortunately very different ideas and values come out of the Puffin publishing house which once had a name for a responsible attitude to children's reading. For example in *The Forest of Doom* by Ian Livingstone there is an emphasis on horror and sadism which is typical. In one place the reader is expected to envisage his invasion and possession by an evil spirit: 'You try to take the crown off your head but it will not move. It is evil and has found a new host in you. Gradually your features change as you adopt the shape and colour of a Fire Demon. Your new destiny is determined and your adventure ends here.'

The death of the reader is frequently enacted, usually very unpleasantly. In one book the reader is transfixed by a harpoon which protrudes bloodily from his stomach. In the same book, black-cowled figures take part in a type of black mass: ' . . . He hands you the chalice and you have to drink. It is human blood, cursed in death's name. It curdles in your stomach and you are seized with a palsy.'

The text is heavily larded with blood, mutilation, witchcraft, torture, beheaded clones that dissolve into pools of purple liquid and blood-sucking Tangleweed!

Although healthy children will no doubt cope with these books unscathed, they do present dangers. Fantasy is a powerful medium for transmitting ideas at conscious and subconscious level; psychiatrists and paediatricians already have had experience of patients suffering from emotional and psychological damage produced by exposure to violent and occult material, and these books form only part of the barrage of cruelty and obscenity from the world around.

First, they invite the reader's total involvement by their matey style ('Isn't this exciting?') and hair-raising adventures.

Second, they may have a de-sensitising influence. They represent the infliction of pain as a source of pleasure, and encourage an attitude of callousness to human suffering by presenting it as a matter of indifference whether you choose to help someone in need, or ignore him.

. . . you hear a low moan . . . you see the ugly sight of a huge man with muscles like knotted iron staked out to the ground. The man is naked except for a small loin cloth and his skin is badly blistered. His face and chest show signs of cruel torture . . . If you wish to cut him free, turn to 128. If you want to leave him in his agony turn to 394.

Third, some of the practices and incantations described have a core of authenticity and offer an education in a type of knowledge which is dangerous to possess and is expressly forbidden in the Bible. We are a far cry from 'whatsoever things are true and lovely and of good report'.

Fourth, evil is on the whole made rather more interesting than goodness.

Children's reading presents parents with the problem of finding time for essential evaluation, but this must be done, for too heavy a diet of sadism, witchcraft and evil can destroy the moral sense of the next generation and condition them to accept as normal practices and behaviour which any civilised society would condemn.

Remember to offer your children good alternative reading in the fantasy genre: George Macdonald's fairy tales, J.R.R. Tolkien's *Lord of the Rings*, C.S. Lewis's *Narnia Chronicles* and more recent excellent publications: *Hagbane's Doom* and *Gublak's Greed* by John Houghton; *The Tower of Geburah* and *The Iron Sceptre* (Kingsway); *The Dragon King* trilogy and space-age fantasy, *Dream Thief* by Stephen Lawhead (Lion), and so on.

Sex and love, marriage and family life

On the whole the media give a poor view of family life and a misleading idea of what relationships between the sexes ought to be. If it is a comedy programme, infidelity is seen as a huge joke; or else the married relationship is one of jealousy and suspicion. It is rare to see a marriage in which the partners are unselfish, forgiving and truly loving. The ladies of the soap operas are portrayed in countless expensive outfits perfecting techniques for manipulating their menfolk and the plots usually depend on intrigue, exchanging marriage partners and leaping in and out of bed. Teenagers who have no stable family background can hardly be expected to take the institution seriously.

Feminists complain that women are always portrayed in a domestic role in the media. This is almost exclusively true of advertising, which does in fact come closer to reality than the programmes themselves, where the home-making woman is rarely given sympathetic treatment, or indeed any treatment at all. Most female characters are bitchy women, scoring points off their husbands, glad to take the men down a peg. Nor does the portrayal of the male promote the idea of marriage, since there are so few caring, supportive husbands on the screen.

Children's stories, teenage magazines and novels

Speaking in general terms, teenage children will not find a more helpful portrayal of marriage or of relationships between the sexes in the current young adult novels and teenage magazines.

The boys' magazines (for example, *Eagle* and *Scream*, *Tiger*, *Warlord*, *Spiderman*) give the impression that there is a great gulf fixed between the sexes, for the female side scarcely appears in them. Their absorption with battle scenes, science fiction and football allows for no portrayal of family life and gives no hint that communication between the sexes is possible. On the other hand there is something to be said in their favour. They often make moral points and a lot of their stories are about the battle between good and evil, (usually in terms of fantasy or science fiction) in which the 'good' side – no mistaking with names such as Heroic Autobots, Evil Decepticons or 'The evil warlord Baron Ironblood' – invariably wins. This can make some contribution to moral development, although the fact that the 'good' side wins is of less value here than that the hero should be both truly noble and compellingly attractive.

The adolescent quest is not for virtue: 'Do I want to be good?' It is for identity: 'Who do I want to be like?' It is the fact that the hero becomes an example to admire and imitate that is formative in building morality into the sense of identity. 'The inner and outer struggles of the hero imprint morality on him' (Bettelheim). The boys' comics often do portray hero-figures who act with courage, initiative and honour. Even though in real life we are all ambivalent, and these are cardboard cut-outs, their lack of 'roundness' is more than compensated for by their value as models to boys at that particular age when they crave, indeed need, someone to hero-worship. It is just possible that the pattern of a man who does not lie or deceive or take advantage of someone weaker may carry over into their adult life and sexual relationships.

The pop magazines read by both girls and boys are a different matter, for in featuring so many homosexual groups whose music carries lyrics with dubious or perverted sexual overtones, they are an unhealthy influence.

The girls' magazines are in direct contrast to the boys' in that they give the impression that sexual relationships are the be-all and end-all of life. We would be living in a fantasy world ourselves if we did not expect romance to be the chief interest of teenage girls. It is sad, therefore, that this avidly read material with all the realism of the photo-story, should give such a low view of love. There is less of deep affection founded on trust and respect than of instant physical attraction followed very rapidly by sexual activity: 'the next minute we were tumbling on to the sofa, breathlessly peeling off each other's clothes, and making wild, glorious, abandoned love' (*Loving*). The fella is an object to be grabbed before someone else gets him. All other topics – fashion, music, health and beauty – are subservient to this over-riding theme.

The real life settings encourage the readers to identify with the situation, and indeed they might find themselves facing some of the problems; but the heroines make unworthy role-models. Pre-marital sex seems to be regarded as the norm. It is true that some of the stories encourage decent behaviour by suggesting that deception can backfire on you, or that a warm, caring, honest nature can be more attractive than bitchy manoeuvres or seductive advances. Moreover their problem pages usually support family life by discouraging affairs with married men and by referring the readers back to their parents for mutually agreed guidelines on dating.

Their libertarian attitudes are dangerous, but they are not salacious: their very superficiality makes them potentially less harmful than the teenage novels on the market, many of which are written with psychological insight and with literary skill. Moreover the object of the producers of the comics, as they freely admitted in a TV interview with anxious mothers, is simply to make money. More ominously, behind the current trends in the young adult novel, there are socio-political aims.

Children's literature has become a battleground for all those who hope, by pressurising the young, to influence the future. Libertarian and homosexual lobbies are also very vocal at present in educational circles. They propagate their ideas aggressively in letters and articles printed in journals for teachers and librarians and publications about children's literature. The Gay Liberation campaign aims to convince children that homosexuality is healthy and that lesbian relationships are normal by promoting novels about 'gay' relationships; while the libertarian critics urge that descriptions of sexual activity are an adolescent 'need.' This is not literary criticism; the novel is not the place for material that belongs in sex education books. After all, if you want a detailed account of the internal combustion engine you choose an automobile manual. They maintain that the last taboo in teenage fiction is an adequate, accurate and sustained description of the sex act and that this should now be broken. They are confusing 'needs' with 'wants' and ignoring the fact that some taboos are necessary for health and social reasons.

You should keep an eye on what your children are reading, for you may be astonished at what passes as children's literature today. You will find vivid descriptions of seduction and sexual activity (for example, *Edith Jackson* by Rosa Guy and *The First of Midnight* by Marjorie Darke); permissive attitudes (*Goodnight, Prof Love* by John Rowe Townsend); titillating and salacious passages (*Basketball Game* by Julius Lester); homosexuality (*In the Tent* by David Rees and *I'll Get There, It'd Better be Worth the Trip* by John Donovan); swearing and blasphemous language (*Come to Mecca* by Farukh Dhondy). It is becoming perfectly normal to find God's name used in jest or anger, in a way that would have been unheard of a decade ago. The frequency with which abortion appears (*My Darling, My Hamburger* by Paul Zindel), although it probably has what the author intends to be a discouraging portrayal, makes it seem that this devastating experience can be shrugged off like a cold. This material, *possibly* labelled teenage or young adult fiction, will be in the children's section of the public library, and therefore available for the child of any age who can read.

Should we exercise censorship? The literary scene was very different when I was trained as a teacher, when the idea was to give children anything that might encourage them to read. Since then I have changed my mind. First, because I had no idea then that children's literature could include such corrupting influences. But also because I now perceive the hypocrisy of the libertarian stance. Censorship on grounds of racism, sexism, class, and so on is not only approved, it is demanded; while censorship on literary or moral grounds is condemned. Librarians and teachers can censor what they offer and parents can do as they think fit, but there can be no guarantee that our children will not at some time read a book that would not meet our own critical standard. If that happens it is important that children should not fear angry rebuke or feel that they have to be secretive about what they read. The home must be a place where there is a climate of openness in all things. Where books are discussed, all kinds of life issues come up, and the major criterion must always be, 'What is this book doing to my child?'

It is unfortunate that the libertarian element in children's fiction is not counter-balanced by a portrayal of ordinary families with responsible parents; broken families and irresponsible, positively vicious parents predominate. This may well reflect society, but such a negative portrayal of parenting means that children who are deprived of mother and father models in real life are also deprived of them in their books. It may have consequences in a self-perpetuating pattern.

The cult of cruelty

We must beware that we do not bring our children up in an environment tailormade to produce monsters. We are becoming desensitised to scenes of cruelty and violence because we see so much on TV. Even documentaries sometimes dwell on the macabre as though it were pleasurable, but the fact that we accept it passively does not make it right.

At one time there would have been a public outcry at the idea of exposing children to an exhibition as degrading as the London Dungeon. According to Richard Wilkins writing with dry humour in *ACT NOW*, it aims to attract school parties by advertising itself as 'a unique and thought-provoking exhibition of British medieval torture, disease and witchcraft.' Under the guise of providing historical information and an hour or two of innocent fun, it presents to the wide-open fresh young minds of the visitors such delights as 'burnings, brandings, disembowellings, impalings, and various kinds of torture, urging them to drink in the splendours of human atrocity . . . Here the children can see that adults are prepared to spend and make money in the merchandising of human cruelty. The fact that adults lavish such skill and care in re-presenting human hideousness shows that it must be good.' They may 'experience awe and wonder at an unfortunate fellow being boiled alive' or witness Thomas Becket 'in full pontificals having his head split open while cathedral plainsong continues undisturbed'. Richard Wilkins has labelled it 'the most preposterous collection of mental garbage to which people of all ages have legal access . . . We should feel outraged by the flagrant commercialisation of human beings' degraded fascinations.'

We should, however, be encouraged by the fact that the spiritually unhealthy Devil's Cavern – 'a display of writhing figures variously copulating (if that is the right word for a crowd scene) under the orders of a twelve-foot animated Devil' – was closed following a critical article in *Family* magazine. A letter alerting a Christian journal may be the parents' best means of counter-attack to any further manifestations of the cult of cruelty.

Video nasties

The London Dungeon is only one symptom of a current preoccupation. The appetite for cruelty reaches its most potentially dangerous level in those video films of such depravity that they have been condemned for public viewing by the Director of Public Prosecutions.

No one can tell how far-reaching the consequence may be of the widespread viewing of these films by children in their most impressionable years. The reports of the Parliamentary Group Video Enquiry suggests that they may be more individually damaging and socially disruptive than has hitherto been realised, for they are making their mark on the young at a time when other factors are combining to make society unstable and to shake children's security.

The video cassette recorder is a totally new phenomenon with enormous implications for the human race. It is now owned by nearly half the population of Britain and a staggering one-third of children under eight have seen one or more of the films now known as 'video nasties'.

It is difficult to establish a direct link between the viewing of violence and violent behaviour; other variables must be taken into account, such as the increased level of violence in society and the prevalence of insecure homes. However, some of the things that teachers have reported and children have said suggest that there is such a link. For children, seeing often is doing. One teacher told me that ghoulish scenes from videos such as *The Evil Dead* were favourite topics of conversation on the journey to and from the swimming baths. Another wrote, 'The children tend to revel in and see as humorous acts of violence that they have seen. One overhears them discussing the fact that they watch such films with relish.'

Horror films are particularly popular, and the video has

114

the advantage, children say, that they can play the gory bits over and over again. Not surprisingly, these scenes remain in the mind. Some children have complained of being unable to rid themselves of the mental pictures for days, and teachers report that the horrific imagery is reproduced in their school work – in art and creative writing, in imaginative play, with the language and violence in inter-personal relationships. Case histories from psychiatrists, doctors, psychologists and the NSPCC confirm this evidence of the damaging effect of feeding the emergent personality on large doses of visual sado-masochistic material. The immediate results may be in excessive fears, nightmares, bed-wetting, and other symptoms of deep anxiety. These may not last long where the children are healthy and where they are supported by a wise, secure and loving home. However, where they are already emotionally disturbed or temperamentally nervous there may be permanent damage. Those who are violent by nature are more likely to be incited to imitation.

Although there are many factors contributing to the current wave of social violence, many teachers, psychiatrists and social workers believe that this new factor may be playing a contributary part. Boys and girls have always quarrelled and fought, defied their parents and been destructive. Teachers well know this, but the changes they comment on are more fundamental. Instead of fair fights there is the brutal ganging up on a single victim; there is a delight in the macabre and in cruelty. Attacks on teachers are on the increase, and one wrote that to supervise the playground is a nightmare. These reports suggest that we are beginning to create a generation of children *with a different set of values from previous ones*.

In their thorough review of research into the long-term effects of television viewing as a moral influence Liebert and Poulos (1976) state that:

. . . television is a moral teacher and a powerful one. Contemporary television entertainment is saturated with violence and related anti-social behaviour and lessons which have a clear, and by most standards, adverse effect on young viewers' development and behaviour.

The same is obviously true, and to a far more potent degree, of the 'video nasty'. Moreover the appetite for sado-masochism grows by being fed on. Soldiers are immunised to the horrors of combat by a programme of films showing shots of bombardments, mutilated corpses and so on. This is what is being done to the rising generation.

Often there are sexual or occult elements in addition to the sadism. There always has been violence in the child's world of imagination, for example in nursery rhymes, fairy tales and westerns, but any parent can see that there is a world of difference between Cock Robin's death, or *Bluebeard*, the grisliest fairy tale, or even a battle between Red Indians and cowboys, and such a video as *The Evil Dead*, where:

Playing the tape released evil forces. Cheryl is molested by possessed vines entwining her body, ripping away her clothing and apparently raping her, a branch entering her vagina . . . Cheryl, now possessed, stabs her friend and is beaten into a cellar. Shelley also comes under demonic influence and attacks Ash and Scott with an axe. They use the axe to chop her to pieces and a hand is eaten. They bury the apparently still living remains. Linda then becomes possessed and attacks the two men, inflicting stab wounds and tearing the flesh from one of the men's legs. Ash kills Linda in a struggle, but she erupts from the grave and has to be decapitated with a spade . . . Two demons repeatedly assault Ash and one has his eye gouged out . . .

Fairy tales, folk tales, historical novels and westerns are all distanced from the child's world by their setting. These

116

video films are terrifyingly close to the street, playground and bedroom of the child's own environment.

A disturbing type of writing has entered with the young adult novel and seems to be becoming increasingly popular. By the use of expressions such as 'cracking bone increased Joe's desire to inflict pain' or that on seeing blood spurting he 'felt greatness descend upon him', it seeks to titillate the senses by making cruelty attractive. Its aim is to arouse sadistic pleasure. In such writings, as in the video nasty, we are often invited to view the act from the perspective of the perpetrator – to participate, as it were, and to identify not with a model of heroism or morality, but with a pattern of revolting viciousness. Parents who allow their children to view such films or read such books are offering them criminals and psychopaths on which to shape their self-image.

It became apparent during the survey conducted by the Parliamentary Group Video Enquiry that parental attitudes have a significant influence on what their children watch, and that while there are parents who are indifferent to their children's viewing habits, there are others who do not realise that their children are seeing these films, because they are shown at a friend's house. An eight-year-old girl known to me went to tea with some friends and there was shown a film about demon possession. She could not sleep for many nights and was terrified to go to bed, screaming that an evil spirit was trying to enter her body. Eventually, after much prayer on her behalf, she was released from this fearsome experience by laying on of hands.

It was found that where parents were protective and vigilant, keeping an eye on friendships and visits, comparatively few children had been exposed. Where they were very liberal in their attitudes to the films, and left children without supervision or guidelines, correspondingly larger numbers have watched violent videos.

In families where there was a history of violent behaviour or child abuse, it was often the case that violent

117

videos were popular. Where the parents enjoy such films it is almost impossible to protect children either from their damaging effects or from the further effect on violently-disposed parents. Legislation can only be really effective if it bans video nasties, not simply from children's viewing, but also from adults.

The phenomenon of the video nasty coincides with and contributes to a period when violence is increasing at all levels – internationally, socially and in the home. Moreover, those institutions which have provided the framework of our life as a community, that is the family, the economy, education, law and government and the Church (including all Christian denominations), are all enduring schism, upheaval and change. It is a bewildering time for adults as well as children. If anything is to be learnt from the survey it is that libertarians, in their demand for freedom, must not be allowed to destroy the value system which has hitherto provided a healthy, secure environment for our children. As parents we must speak up whenever we have the opportunity. We must make our homes stable and inviolable. We must give our children that security which can hold them steady against the disorienting pressures of change, and impervious to the behavioural code of violence which is currently injected into our lives.

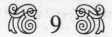

9

Broken Boughs

When the bough breaks the cradle will fall.
Anon

The family is the child's greatest source of security. Any
threat or influence from outside, however menacing, can
be faced from within that framework. Death and divorce
alike both shatter the framework. They are among the
most destabilising experiences that a child may meet.
However, something may be done to lessen the damage
if, in spite of their own problems and pain, parents are
able to keep in view what is happening to the children.

In either experience the children lose a parent and all
that that parent meant in terms of affection and security.
At the same time they may lose their home, their familiar
places, school and friends; for both death and divorce
may bring financial loss and changing circumstances. If
the remaining parent has to turn out to work it may mean
losing much of his or her companionship as well.

The greater loss

But there is a significant difference. In spite of death's
finality, divorce may be the more harrowing experience.
Looked at from the children's point of view, a divorce
means that one of their parents has chosen to leave them.
This is a demeaning thought, very different from death,
and hard for a child to understand. No one, they can see,
can help dying, but it is hard to accept that mummy or
daddy has deliberately walked out. Things can be better
where the children can continue to keep in touch with
both parents, and where they can be reassured that whatever has happened between their mother and father, they
themselves are still loved and valued by both of them.

This means, too, that they still keep the grandparents and aunts and uncles on both sides.

Unfortunately, where a parent has left the first partner in order to marry someone else, it is highly probable that eventually all contact with the children of the first marriage will be lost. Visits may be kept up for a while, then come to a full stop as a new home and new family take all the time and attention that once belonged to those abandoned first children:

> I thought how like bereavement a divorce can be. I was on my own with Caroline (aged three) and Justin when we separated, her daddy visiting about every third Saturday. When one week he had again not showed up she was upset and said, 'Daddies don't do that, I'm not calling him Daddy.'

It is bad enough to know that Daddy does not want to spend his time with you – worse to realise that he is devoting it to another child.

Whatever the circumstances may be, it is best to avoid anger when talking about it with the children and to avoid running the other partner down. The less negative feelings displayed the better. Leave the children something to respect and value in the one who has gone, for the sake of their own self-respect. On the other hand, when a parent has died people sometimes go to the other extreme, idealising the dead parent and giving the children an impossible example to live up to. This is not very helpful either.

Truth not mystery

Death has no real meaning for small children; their concept of death develops slowly, in line with their intellectual, emotional and spiritual growth. Under the age of four, a child would find it difficult to accept the finality of death and is likely to cherish the futile hope that one day Daddy will return. It was a four-year-old who said, 'We will bury my doggy now, and in the spring, when the flowers come back, he will come back, too.' About the age of nine most children become aware that death is final and universal, and that one day they themselves may die; and by the time they enter secondary school they are capable of exploring all the many aspects of death and dying.

It may also take a long time for the full impact of divorce to sink in, and a child may hope unrealistically for a long time that there will be a reconciliation. On the other hand it may be that for several years before the separation the children have sensed the tension and hostility between their parents, even if there have not been open quarrels. A five-year-old told her grandmother, 'I don't believe mummy and daddy love each other any more.' Such knowledge makes a child grow old beyond her years.

It is a great mistake to try and deceive children with half truths and made up stories. It is not always easy to tell the truth. We would all like to shield children from tragedy. Many children of divorcing parents are told almost nothing about what is going on, and the child whose life is changing dramatically has to make what sense of it he can. But a lack of honesty creates a feeling of mystery and insecurity. Those who are told the truth and kept in the picture adapt more easily. Otherwise they may weave their own erroneous fantasies around the situation. For instance it may be the father who has walked out, but arriving with presents at the week-end, he appears far more appealing than the rather jaded mother who has had to struggle with the problems of the week on her own.

For bereaved children, too, the truth is best. Their future will be affected by the way in which this experience is handled.

My mother died when I was three: and although I am now thirty-eight and a mother myself this has coloured my whole life, giving me a fundamentally pessimistic view of the world, which nothing can shift. I don't know whether a different handling of my emotions as a child would have made a difference to me, but I suppose it might. My father, from the best of motives and a desire to spare me, never told me that my mother had died and never spoke of her. This, I'm sure is wrong. Before anything else a young child must be allowed to grieve in full (*Children, Death and Bereavement*).

The painful news should if possible be broken to the children by someone close, with every message of reassurance that a lot of cuddling and loving can give.

When I told my children their father had died I had both of them sitting on my mother's settee with their Grandad by them in the middle. I told them he was up in heaven with God and that he would always be watching us as our life went by . . . then we just kissed and cuddled. My father explained how the whole family would look after us and make sure we were all right, which helped a lot (*Children Death and Bereavement*).

Response

A child's response to bereavement or divorce will be affected by his age, stage of intellectual and emotional development, background and upbringing, and also by the circumstances. The shock, for instance, to his little girls, when their father fell from his bike and was crushed by a lorry, has made the five-year-old turn back to baby ways, seeking security. Two other little girls, aged four and six, whose Daddy died after a long spell in hospital, had become more used to his not being at home, though of course they sorrowed for him. Older children can think about their feelings more objectively. A twelve-year-old said, 'In some ways it's easier for me that my father died the way he did – all of a sudden – instead of having to go through a lot of pain and suffering.' While a fifteen-year-old felt that the long-drawn out trauma of watching his mother die of cancer had prepared him for her death: 'It didn't hurt less. I was just able to stand the pain more.'

A true Christian faith, which offers to the lonely child

a reunion with Daddy in heaven, can make a fundamental difference to the bereavement. A seven-year-old, whose father was killed by falling from a ladder, wrote from the perspective of manhood, 'When my father died, to me he had gone to be with Jesus Christ, and that made all the difference.'

Children of divorce also meet varied experiences. The separation may have been managed calmly and amicably or it may have followed a series of blazing rows. But in any event the children lose a role model and this may affect their ability to make satisfactory relationships as they grow up. A girl who is deprived of her father during the years when she is forming her concepts of how to relate to the opposite sex, loses her mental picture of the man she might one day wish to marry. Research tells us that adolescent boys who lose their father's example, authority and support suffer most and may become very depressed or perhaps rebellious and delinquent.

Guilt, anger, rebellion, neuroses

Ironically, children, the innocent victims of tragedy or of adult failure, are prone to blame themselves for what has happened. Young children see the world as revolving entirely round themselves. A four-year-old whose mother dies may believe that she 'went away' because he was naughty, or that she died because he was angry with her for something which she did or did not do – that his 'powerful' anger has killed her. According to this 'magical thinking' he is guilty of his mother's death. A girl whose father has left home may think, 'He didn't love me – I'm not lovable – no one will love me.' A boy who adores his mother may believe that it was his fault that the father walked out. Guilty feelings may be complicated by shock, sorrow, and even by anger directed at the absent parent for no longer being available to fulfil the child's needs and wishes. Older children and teenagers may suffer agonies of remorse over memories of disobedience and rebellion.

Children do not always show on the outside what they are feeling on the inside, Parents need to be aware that even an apparently stable and unmoved child may be undergoing turmoil within and this may produce problems later. A recent survey of children interviewed several years after their parents had parted revealed that a third had never recovered from the trauma. Likewise the deep impact of childhood bereavement may not show until some other event in adulthood acts like a catalyst to trigger a psychotic disorder or emotional problem of some kind.

Children's reactions are very varied, and where they are not able to express their feelings in words, they may show them in body language. The effects of bereavement and divorce may show in behaviour that reverts to baby-hood, thumb-sucking, bedwetting, temper tantrums; it may produce nightmares, nervousness or digestive upsets. It may lead to various sorts of delinquent behaviour, stealing or vandalism. A five-year-old Kenyan Asian girl whose father died after she had been in this country for only a year and who could speak little English, must have found the bereavement doubly unsettling. The confusion in her mind could be seen in her constant comments that 'The police had taken Daddy away', that 'Daddy is in the ground but soon he will be coming back' and 'My daddy doesn't like me'. This child was found with school and other children's property. Her teacher wrote:

> I feel this behaviour is her way of compensating for her loss in some way. I tell her why she must not take things that do not belong to her and I try to see that she has a painting or a piece of work that she has done to take home. I feel that the child needs time to come to terms with her loss but I will keep a close eye on this tendency to taking things (*Children, Death and Bereavement*).

One mother of teenagers whose husband was lost at sea felt that the loss of a father comes particularly hard on the adolescent. Soon after the drowning, her two sons, aged fourteen and sixteen, were arrested for making nuisance calls on neighbours; and during the few days while they were waiting for definite news of their Dad, the eldest boy 'would ride his bike carelessly round the streets, thinking that if he were to be killed it would save his dad. His death in exchange for his father's life.' She wrote, 'There seems to be plenty of help available for small children but possibly one expects teenagers to cope. This may not be so. The teenage years are a traumatic period anyway without coping with the death of a parent.'

These experiences highlight the need for informing family doctors and teachers about any such deeply disturbing family affairs. Not only may they keep the sort of wise and kindly watching brief as the little Kenyan Asian girl's teacher, but they may exercise a discreet control over the way such children are treated by their peers. They may also advise calling in a professional counsellor if they feel such help is needed.

School

The Headmistress of a church primary school told me of her disquiet at the large proportion of her pupils who, in this comfortable middle-class area were 'eating their hearts out' because their parents had separated and the children, torn between the two of them and loving both, were 'beside themselves with grief'. She did not mince her words. These children of broken homes, not yet eleven years old, were full of despair, some even suicidal. For such children the school environment must provide stability, concern and support.

A seven-year-old had the unsettling experience of being tossed to and fro from one parent to the other. At school he became extremely aggressive, bullying the other children. He 'wanted to make them sad'. Asked why, he replied, 'I wanted my mummy to come back.'

Within the school situation it is possible at least to provide understanding, and the listening ear. And sometimes the children help each other. Alan, a disruptive boy from a problem home palled up with a boy whose father had died, and shouldered the responsibility of creating a good environment for him. Alan's difficulties began to fall away in his concern for the bereaved boy and, in helping someone else, he grew up a lot. The role of protector matured him.

In one class a pupil's father had been killed in recent riots and the teacher felt that it would be best to speak to them before the boy returned. 'Do children go to funerals?' they wanted to know. 'Where is the grave?' 'Will Colin be crying?' They were concerned and eager to help. The teacher told them that God is our loving Father and that he cares particularly for people who are sad. 'Shall we pray together?' she asked, and the children were glad to join in doing something that they saw as a positive act. Prayer is as valid in the experience of children as it is for adults. The teacher then warned the class not to press Colin for details of his father's death, but if he wanted to talk about it he must be allowed to do so.

Talk is therapeutic for distressed children and sometimes they will talk more easily with their friends than with adults. For older children writing may take its place. A ten-year-old whose father had left home wrote a poem about himself which finished, 'Most of all he loves his mum and dad.' He also made a Valentine for the absent father. A fifteen-year-old whose father had died of a heart attack after they had had a row was plagued by remorse. He found no peace until his teacher encouraged him to write a letter to his dead father, explaining his point of view and asking for forgiveness. Children should be encouraged not to bottle up their sorrow. Sometimes photographs can make unobtrusive starting points for memories, and books too can be helpful. They may provide an escape from present pain, or they may help a child to come to terms with the bereavement by exploring in story the feelings of a character who also has experienced the sorrow and questionings, as in Patricia St John's *The Tanglewood's Secret*. C. S. Lewis's fantasy *The Last*

Battle and Oscar Wilde's fairy tale *The Selfish Giant* communicate an insight into the spiritual meaning of death.

Ritual

Children as young as seven years old, maybe younger, should be allowed to attend a parent's funeral if they want to. One boy said, 'My father died when I was nearly seven. We boys were asked if we wished to go to the funeral. My brother is now glad that he chose not to do so, but I am glad that I did.'

A funeral is an occasion when the family sorrow together and find support and comfort in each other's company. The child can feel part of this closely bonded unit, and is not shut out from what is going on. Ritual is a very important element in the lives of children, and the funeral service provides a dignified framework which satisfies this need: but from then on the concern of adults should be to provide a new start and an adequate environment.

Starting again

Once the funeral is over and life begins to gain a semblance of normality, every effort should be made to find interesting activities and new horizons that will take children out of themselves. Pets are rather special to the heart of a lonely child; dogs have a real gift of empathy and children can confide their deepest feelings to their four-footed friends who provide uncritical, sympathetic companionship. Cubs, Scouts and other groups draw children into a community which is independent of parents, while church-based ones such as Crusaders and Campaigners, Climbers and Explorers, are a microcosm of God's family, adding to human companionship a spiritual dimension which can be a real source of strength.

The happiest solution for broken families may be for the remaining parent to find another partner, and so relieve the children of the pressure of feeling that they must try to fill the empty place. Children sometimes feel so responsible for a parent that they forego marriage when they grow up. However, re-marriage must not be an impulsive step or one taken to solve problems of finance or loneliness. Marriage is only a solution if it is right for everyone concerned. There is a worrying trend for marriages following a divorce to again meet with disaster, making a shattering experience for the children. The idea that you can simply replace a parent by finding another partner comes from a lack of understanding of the symbolic importance of individual parents in the life of the child. Seven-year-old Tracey ran away from home taking her four-year-old brother with her because she was so afraid that her family was going to collapse a second time.

The way we relate to children affects their estimate of their own worth. This is a very important factor in the development of personality and we need to be sensitive in our attitude to children bereft of parents. There was a time when by some peculiar malfunction of logic, the children of divorce became included in a general aura of disapproval. This reinforced their sense of rejection and separated them from other children. One spin-off of the proliferation of broken homes is that at least these children are no longer so different. Most churches now have a particular concern for widowed or divorced parents and their children, giving them warmth of friendship and practical help. We must not, however, make the mistake of extending to these children the sort of pitying attitude that can destroy a child's independence and fortitude. Children in general are resilient like thrusting young plants.

Given a kindly environemnt their wounds heal. Sometimes their difficult circumstances bring out fine character traits – fortitude, tenacity and human understanding. They need encouragement, as all children do, and they also need respect and the assurance that they have within themselves the resources they need to face the world.

In spite of all the problems the choice of single parenthood may sometimes be the best adjustment to a difficult situation – better for instance than leaving a child open to physical or sexual abuse, where safety and well-being cannot be guaranteed. Those who find that they have to make such a choice should take courage, for 'The shame of your youth and the sorrows of widowhood will be remembered no more, for your Creator will be your "husband" ' (Isaiah 54.5). The following letter describes such a situation:

I first turned to God when I was being beaten up nearly every evening by my one-year-old son's father, with whom I had been engaged for two years and he didn't want to get married. I got down on my knees one night and turned to God in prayer, and I told him that I was living in sin and I didn't want to go against him any more, and I locked my son's dad out every night, and from then until now I still haven't gone against God.

Myself and my son, Peter, were turned out of the house, and we were put into homeless families, into a little box room, but I felt at peace. At least I had my own key and could lock my few belongings away, and because we were good we were moved first into a flat in a tower block, on the tenth floor. Then one day, students came to our door from a nearby church . . . I asked them what was the prayer to say for my sins to be forgiven through Jesus. As I said that prayer I felt all my sins come away from me and I knew my sins had been forgiven, and I felt as if I were walking on air . . .

When I first became a Christian I felt a bit bad about having a child before getting married, and I mentioned this to my pastor's wife and all she said was, 'Your child is a gift from God,' and as I thought about this I realised that God does answer prayer in mysterious ways because I always wanted to have children. So I thanked God for my son.

Peter is now ten years old, growing up into a fine, strong, Christian boy within the framework of the local church where his mother sings in the choir. He will not know a father's love, but neither will he live under the intolerable pressure of constant bickering and conflict in a home where no love is.

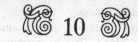

10

Wounded Children

I am horribly punished, even though I have not sinned.
Job

Graham Brown of the Church of England's Children's Society runs a safe house for runaway children. Among their reasons for leaving home he cites: seeking independence, unemployment, personal tensions and intolerable family problems. In the confusing years of adolescence some may have found family ties unbearably restricting, and their search for identity demands that they break away. Others have been wounded by experiences within the home. Of those who are seeking their independence with high hopes of making their way in the world, most are going to meet with disappointment, hardship and maybe despair. The problem is a growing one and a matter of great concern as terrible dangers await these runaways. Some of them fall prey to men waiting at the big urban railway stations for these innocents from the country. Many of them add to the vast and growing numbers of young homeless in London. Voluntary agencies such as Alone in London, Centrepoint, Night Shelter and Boot Night Shelter (in Birmingham) report on the critical nature of the problem and on the fact that those they take in are getting increasingly younger.

Family discord

This is one of the major causes of children leaving home. They can take a certain amount of quarrelling provided they know that underneath there is a firm base of love that is not going to give way. When they see that the home is likely to break up, running away is their wild appeal for help. A ten-year-old wrote about his fears:

Why I wanted to leave home

Before my summer holiday my father found some photos of
my mum's old boy friend. Then he started – he don't like my
mum any more. Last Tuesday at nine o'clock in the morning
I hear my father hit my mum again. Then I knocked at the
door and asked what happened but my father said 'Nothing',
and I heard my mum crying, so I think I wanted to leave this
home. I put my things in my bag and went.

But I thought, 'I can't leave my father and mum,' so I went
back. When I got back to my home my mum saw me. Then
she is really happy and she asked me why I wanted to leave
this family. Then I said, 'Because I don't want to see you two
fighting any more.' Then she said they are not fighting. Then
I said, 'I am not a baby! I can hear you are crying. If you
have something unhappy, tell me. I will tell my father.' And
then she told me.

In this case the boy felt responsible for his parents.
Another boy whose father had left home after a quarrel
actually went after him.

One day I wanted to run away so I made a plan to leave
home. First I would gather all my money that I had at home,
then I would . . . get the bus to Woolwich Ferry and walk to
my dad's block of flats . . .

Often in the news are children who run away for a day
or a night in pique over some grievance, not realising the
agony this makes for parents who think their child has
gone for good. If parents express their anxiety forcefully
when teenagers stay out late and do not say where they
are going they will avoid this misunderstanding.

Cults

Some are lured into the communal life of cults, thinking
they will find something there that they have not found
at home. It may be the closeness that attracts them; for
even in families that have been strongly bonded through
childhood, parents sometimes find themselves unable to

communicate their affection to their teenagers. This can make the insecure adolescent vulnerable to cult offers of love and concern. It may be authority; for although too heavy a hand may produce rebellion, there is also a danger in not providing leadership. The father's role demands both sensitivity and confidence, for youngsters need someone to carry difficult decisions. Here again the cult movements have an appeal, rendering life less complicated for those prepared to submit their will.

We can do something then, to protect children from the cult enticement, by keeping the lines of communication open, by finding undemanding ways of making our love known and by providing a reasonable authority.

Those who become involved with cults are usually warm-hearted, impulsive, yearning for a purpose beyond earthly ambition. Among them sadly are some who have been brought up in Evangelical circles, but who have somehow missed the purpose and fulfilment that Christian dedication could have brought them. They may have found Christianity too 'sensible' and been caught by the impression that cults give of offering entrée to some elite inner knowledge.

The present trend for schools to give equal weight to all religions, and the current media projection of truth as something relative shared by all faiths, make it most important of all to see that our children really know their Bible and understand the unique character of the Christian faith; for otherwise they are left wide open to the misinterpretation and manipulation of those whose aim is to gain control over young minds.

The poverty trap

Inflation, redundancy and unemployment all bring financial pressure and bad housing which also affect the children. Changing economic circumstances, together with the feminist movement, make many women feel impelled to go out to work, and this may take from the home some of its stability and warmth. Donald Carson, of Trinity Evangelical Divinity School has written:

> My parents' combination of commitments kept my mother from working outside the home until we children were largely grown up . . . Say what you will, there is something that breeds security, trust, loyalty and warmth when a child, even a fifteen or sixteen year old, can return home from school, bellow 'Mom' as he comes through the door – and expect an answer.

Although many families are now adjusted to the varied arrangements arising from mother going out to work, trouble may still arise from the reversal of roles and job sharing. It can be confusing for a child who has to decide which parent to go to for which situation, especially if they argue about it. When parents argue about money or behaviour or values or discipline, it burdens the children because they do not know who is right and who is wrong. It is best to wait till they are out of hearing:

Poverty can lead to disastrous consequences, including behavioural and psychiatric problems of both parents and children. Social workers are familiar with the circumstances in which stress on parents results in broken homes, runaway children and child abuse. But long before the state system came into being, voluntary societies had been doing a quiet work to relieve frustration in the inner cities. And many still do. One such is the Shaftesbury Christian Centre run by Tony Powell in which Mrs Dennemont has been involved for the past ten years. She has four children of her own, and she keeps a spare room for a homeless young person, offering the runaway the advantage of independence within a secure, caring, homely environment. She believes that, as a leader within the local church, her particular gift is to show hospitality to all in need, to runaways and to problem families, especially one-parent ones, for she has found that child battering is often a symptom of the frustration and despair to which single parents are subject. Frequently this is the offshoot of loneliness, of having no one to turn to for help, and of impossible housing conditions.

The isolation and impersonality of much inner-city housing, particularly high rise flats, is now recognised as contributing to mental and emotional problems. It also increases racial tension, as we have seen in the riots on the Broadwater estate, Tottenham. Such hostility is not a good beginning for children to grow up in. It does not promote understanding nor help them to make good relationships. Opportunities to play with other children, and learn toleration, are limited.

A recent survey revealed that over nine million people in this country can never afford to have a holiday. They have to go on coping with poverty, unemployment, rundown housing and chronically sick children with no prospect of a break from it at all. It is a great help if they can get away together even for a brief spell. The Family Holiday Association aims to provide such opportunities, to relieve pressure on the parents and children. Case histories they receive from social workers speak of the connection between financial and marital strain, and stress on the children. This is a typical example: Mr Jones has been unemployed for the last four years. Due to the economic climate in the area his prospects of obtaining work are poor . . . Both older children have been a cause for concern. The elder has been experiencing emotional and behavioural problems.

A special child

Difficulties are compounded when there is a mentally or physically handicapped child in the family, as the parents may well be too exhausted to give the other children the attention they need. But attitudes are changing in that there is a wider understanding of the needs of handicapped children and the difficulties that their families face. There have been advances in the provision of care and equipment and in nurturing potential so that life can be made as close to normal as possible, including participation in various sports activities. Down's syndrome children make remarkable progress with the proper stimulation and often show musical aptitude. Following the Warnock Report, it is probable that more disabled children will be receiving a formal education in normal schools.

These are all moves in the right direction, but in themselves they do not reach through to the heart of the problem of handicap. For what is needed is the recognition that handicapped people are nonetheless complete in themselves – their handicap does not diminish them. For the teenager who is asking the question 'Who am I?' handicap makes the creation of a satisfactory self-image a very hard task. The attitude of those around acts like a mirror, and if he sees there a reflection of pity or embarrassment or distaste, the answer to his question will be 'I am a write off'. But the worth of a person is not physical; it is found within. As we have seen in the life of Joni, the American paraplegic artist and writer, handicap accepted in faith with courage, can actually enhance the image and the witness.

Right from the start the way a handicapped baby is received into the family is significant:

> We all looked forward with great excitement to the arrival of Anne's third baby. However, baby Jeanette was born prematurely, terribly handicapped . . . She was blind and deaf, with no voluntary movement, had to be tube fed, was unable to control her body temperature and had fits.
>
> We loved her dearly, sharing her between the two families to ease the burden of care. She brought out an immense gentleness not seen before in the children, who never once even appeared to notice her appearance as anything out of the ordinary . . . and it was a real comfort to know that God had planned Jeanette's life and loved her, just as he planned and loves the other children, that every step of the way she was in his care and keeping, and that it was through our

reactions to this experience that her life would have value and meaning (*Children, Death and Bereavement*).

As with any other child, the challenges that a handicapped child confronts help him to grow, and his independence must be respected. Indeed we may gain more than we give to the handicapped, for sometimes they have access to a deeper spirituality than ours, and I shall not forget the radiant quality of a young man in a wheelchair with his strange rasping voice and shining eyes, who spoke to our fellowship: 'The thing that makes us individuals is not in our peculiar muscles, nor in our wounded nervous systems, but in the God-given self that no infirmity can confine.'

Vicious circle

'I don't know why I did it,' said the father of six-year-old David. He had poured kerosene round his son's bed and set fire to him as he slept. He had been a devoted father but was subject to explosive rages, and his possessive love was unnatural – the obsessional thrust of childhood deprivation. He had, he said, a passion to be the sort of father he had never had. One day in 1983 David received a ninety per cent third degree burn injury. He survived many months of hospitalisation and innumerable operations. Eventually he asked the question.

'I don't know why, Davey,' his mother replied. 'I don't know if we will ever really know. I know that Daddy loves you Davey, but I don't know why he did it.' (This harrowing story can be read in *David*, by Marie Rothenberg and Mel White (Kingsway).)

We don't know why there are so many cases of parental child abuse, especially recently, but we may note that it was in the fifties and sixties that family break-up began to rocket. Parenting is probably the most responsible job that any of us will ever be called upon to do, yet the only preparation that most of us get for it is that we once were children ourselves, and our experiences then will affect the way we treat our children. In an offending parent we shall usually find a neglected, rejected or brutalised child. We begin to be parents in our parents' arms: a history of child abuse in one generation sets up a pattern of abuse through succeeding generations.

Misconceptions

It would be a mistake to suppose that all abusive parents are criminals and psychopaths. They come from all walks of life and not all of them are intentionally cruel. Some of them may be very caring, but deny their children proper nurturing because of some odd theory or deluded religious belief.

It would also be mistaken to believe that all abuse is as shockingly visible as the concentric burn rings from an electric heater on a little girl's bottom: the 'punishment' for a badly timed bowel movement. Emotional damage also makes permanent scars, though they cannot be seen. A child who has been consistently denied parental love and affection, or told repeatedly that he is a nuisance, stupid, unlovable, may well become unlovable and find it impossible to form a satisfactory self-image. It destroys personality.

Prediction

The transmitted factor in child abuse might suggest that it is a hopeless problem. However there are now hopeful signs. Media coverage of the subject has made it easier for parents to come forward for help before they actually injure their children, and in their basic desire to be good parents many opt for the long-term and painful treatment of psychotherapy. More important still, research has shown that it is possible to predict with a high degree of accuracy those parents who are likely to abuse their children, by observing their response to the baby during the first days following the birth. It is then possible to keep an eye on the home and by advice and intervention

138

to help improve relationships between the parents and child.

In crisis situations overwrought parents can now reach advice and professional help, or simply the relief of a listening ear through the hotline scheme run by Parents Anonymous. Many of these parents, having been denied love as children, do not know how to love. For them lay-therapists can offer hope by visiting, talking through problem situations and supplying their need for love and friendship. They also help to lift the load from social workers, many of whom are dangerously overstretched.

Wounded

Many children who have been neglected or damaged by their parents land up in hospital. Their injuries may include bruises, fractures, burns, head and abdominal injuries and the effects of poison. They may be suffering pain, fear, homesickness for the only environment they have known, and even guilt for having been the cause of trouble to their parents.

They stand in great need of reassurance, and to supplement what busy nurses can provide, some hospitals have 'visiting grandmothers', who can spend precious hours in cuddling, listening, comforting and loving these sad children, and helping them to express their fears, grief, anger and deep sense of betrayal.

Not all children will need hospitalisation, but psychological and emotional damage may be severe, hindering the healthy development of personality. Of the younger ones, those who are most disturbed – especially those with language difficulties – may be referred to an individual play-therapist. Some of their experiences may have been so chaotic and horrifying that they cannot separate reality from fantasy and it is important to provide a stable environment for them and to establish a relationship of trust.

School age children may show signs of ill-treatment on their faces or limbs, in their behaviour, creative writing and drama improvisation. They may become hyperactive and aggressive or alternatively withdrawn, depressed and listless. Their reactions may include various types of anti-social behaviour such as we expect from children who have lost a parent or sibling. Indeed, a child may actually have witnessed the death of a brother or sister at the hands of a parent or step-parent and, in addition to the complex feelings of bereavement, be living with fear. Teachers should be on the look-out for any significant details of behaviour or appearance, when bruises appear constantly on faces or limbs, when children seem to be far more accident prone at home than at school and when they give vague, evasive answers about how they came by the tell-tale marks. The Director of the NSPCC commended teachers for their vigilance and co-operation in identifying cases of cruelty.

Home life may be chaotic for abused children and the familiar routine of a well-ordered classroom under a firm and understanding teacher can provide a framework in which an incipient and shaken sense of trust may find roots.

Sexual abuse

The current epidemic of sex crimes against children (ranging from indecent exposure to murder) is now such that it seems probable that one in eleven of the children now in school will be interfered with in some way before reaching adulthood. Life has become very worrying for parents, many of whom are afraid of allowing their children out alone even when they are beginning to be independent at the age of nine or ten.

'The question is,' said my daughter-in-law, when Jonathan was six, 'how can I warn him, without spoiling his outgoingness and friendly personality?' From babyhood, Jonathan has looked on the world as his friend and would chat happily with anyone. At what age should you begin to explain to children that the world is not such a wonderful place after all? We do not want to make our children timid or suspicious, but both girls and boys are in greater danger than ever before, and it seems wise to give some warning at whatever age it becomes likely that they may be out of our personal care for a time.

Children need to be told that there are times when it is right to say 'No' to an adult – 'No' to sweets and rides in cars and secret kisses. No one has the right to interfere with their body, especially those parts that are covered by their bathing costume. That is private. But it is better not to mention any connection with sex as that could lead to problems later. If someone ever does touch or kiss them and tell them to keep it secret, they must not do so – they must straight away tell someone about it. They must also be warned against anyone trying to grab them – to be wary of cars slowing down near them, ready to scream and yell, to kick and run.

In sheep's clothing

Michelle Elliot, who has been going into our schools with the Child Assault Prevention Programme from Ohio, thinks we should warn children as young as three years old. Indirectly, I believe that some fairy tales can help, suggesting obliquely that in the world everything is not always what it seems and that there are dangers. It was with just such a motive that Perrault wrote the original *Red Riding Hood*, to warn young girls at court of the wolves who surrounded them. It is useless, however to warn children only against 'strangers', since the danger may come from the nice man in the sweet shop or even from a relative. It is also useless to warn them against 'bad men' for they do not know who is good and who is bad, and the offender may appear perfectly respectable and act normally. They should be on their guard, and also be taught appropriate self-defence tactics.

After-effects

A single incident of a non-violent kind may carry no after-effects, provided the child is given full reassurance and the parents also receive sympathetic support. But forcible sexual abuse and child rape may require therapeutic treatment over a long period, not only for the victim, but also perhaps for the whole family who may be suffering shock.

Under the age of five, nightmares, bedwetting and clinging behaviour may indicate sexual abuse for which help may be needed from a doctor or therapist. It may also fall within the scope of a nursery school teacher to provide the settling and loving support that will allow the child to work through the experience. In school-age children the signs may be depression, lack of concentration, truancy, hysteria and talk of running away or suicide. If it continues it can rob them of their childhood and drive them to drugs, making them literally tired of living. It denies them control over their own bodies and may seriously affect their adult sexual relationships, making it impossible for them to find stable married happiness.

The NSPCC have reported that in 1985 sexual child abuse increased by over ninety per cent; regrettably incest appears to be more common than was thought. It may include any members of the family – brother/sister, mother/son, even grandparents. It is obviously very difficult to obtain evidence about incest, but it is imperative that the public should be alert to the situation, for children should be given every possible protection from the emotional and psychological damage it causes, and from its medical and social dangers which have made it taboo in all civilised communities.

On a wall in Frankston, Australia, someone has chalked the words, 'Is this what they call incest, Daddy?' Such is a child's innocence and vulnerability, to a parent in particular; and it is not uncommon for incest to begin with a loving relationship that goes wrong. Typical of offending parents is the inability to control their impulses, and also a tendency to confuse their role. They fail to draw the normal distinction between parental affection and passion, between the natural sort of cuddles that we

142

all enjoy with our children and too close an intimacy with a developing child. Common sense should be enough but even among morally upright and intelligent people the record shows that there have been some extraordinary lapses.

It is obvious that financial constraints and inadequate housing, where all the family share one room or several children sleep together with no privacy, can create situations where temptation is powerful.

In some cases the father is domineering and authoritarian, jealously restricting his daughter's social life, especially where boy-friends are concerned, and warning or bribing her into secrecy. Such children live under terrible pressure, unable to seek help, fearing that to reveal the situation would destroy the family. Sometimes a daughter will forgive a father who offended against her, but not the mother who failed to protect her. Her plight may only become known if she becomes pregnant or develops venereal disease or takes to drugs or prostitution.

The long-term effects of incest are devastating: some victims become withdrawn, some suicidal, and all will be burdened by guilt, with very low self-esteem and feelings of confusion regarding their sexuality.

Protection

The protection of our children must be the concern of the whole community – police, parents and neighbours – as it is with Neighbourhood Watch. We must ensure that arrangements for collecting them from school are watertight, perhaps fixing a code word to identify genuine collectors. If we see children out alone on the streets at night, or know they have been left alone in the house, we should alert the police. We must not be afraid to get involved if we see someone approaching a child in a way that looks suspicious; and we must be much more careful about allowing them to go around the houses for Hallowe'en, Guy Fawkes, bob-a-job, charity sponsorship and carols. Recently there have been cases of girls assaulted by men they first met when collecting for school charity efforts.

Teenagers need especially careful guidelines about behaviour because of their greater independence, emotional instability and longing for romantic attachments. This is difficult because girls often become very secretive about their boy-friends and dating; they are not particularly amenable to advice, and tend to think they know all the answers.

Rape

All women are in danger of being raped regardless of age or innocence: it is not a sexual crime, but one of violence and hatred, and the incidence is escalating fast. Girls are sometimes reluctant to report an attack for fear of being accused unjustly of having 'asked for it', and even though powerless to resist they will feel guilty and ashamed. But it is important to see that they can receive counselling therapy as well as any medical attention needed.

Initially they may be too shocked to be able to express their feelings, but as with bereavement, gentle encouragement to share the experience is the best therapy. Above all, believe the girl's story. Assure her that a virgin before rape is just as much a virgin after, and so help to rebuild her shattered self-image. It is counter-productive to comment 'If only you had come home when we said . . .' or 'How many times have we told you not to cross the heath at night?'

Rape is a harrowing experience for the whole family, especially the father, bringing feelings of overwhelming rage and helpless self-recrimination for having been unable to protect her. It needs a united effort to support and reassure one another, and to seek counselling help for other members.

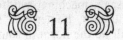

11

Joining the Flock

Feed my lambs.
Jesus

The balance is tricky between pressurising children into
church attendance, maybe premature Christian commitment, and allowing them to grow up without adequate
spiritual armour in a largely pagan environment. 'I don't
go to church now – my parents made me go three times
on Sunday and to umpteen week day meetings, and
turned me off.' Once a common protest. Less so now.
Here is another unhappy reminiscence:

> Sunday School was at ten o'clock and then the children were
> marched to church for the 11 a.m. service. The services were
> long in those days. All the psalms set for the day. Sometimes
> we were not home until nearly one o'clock. From a tiny tot
> I was at that service. Sitting still and being quiet. Not all the
> running about and noise we get nowadays. I amused myself
> by turning the fingers of my gloves inside out and then turning
> them back again. When I was about four or five I would
> scream on a Sunday morning as I did not want to go.

Sausages

'The school had me "done" when I was fourteen – just a
lot of mumbo-jumbo!' is another not uncommon assess-
ment of the practice of having children confirmed when
they reach a certain age. At one school the Headmaster
wrote a standard letter to parents of boys in the fourth
year informing them that their sons were due to be put
forward for Confirmation. A reply came back from one
parent: 'Dear Sir, My son was "done" last year, but if
you want to "do" him again this year, I have no objec-

145

tion.' This 'sausage machine syndrome' is generally discredited in churches, homes and schools nowadays, though it may still be the norm in some places.

Orientation

A fundamental shift has now been made in the Church's approach. The Church of England is now considering allowing children to take Communion before they are confirmed in order to give a more relaxed attitude towards Confirmation. There is a new orientation towards the young, to make them welcome and at ease, recognising their innate spirituality without in any way imposing adult ideas on them. Prams in the aisle and push chairs in the creche are concrete illustrations of the fact that serious consideration is given to the very young; from the earliest years it is now usual to make appropriate provision for children's spiritual and intellectual development. It is an attitude which has been inspired and encouraged by those with responsibility for training the clergy. Many theological colleges build child development courses and school experience into their curriculum. In his *All About Children*, the children's evangelist, John Inchley, argues the need, when talking to children about spiritual matters, to use language which they can understand. In *Children of the King*, Ron Buckland points out that when children make a decision to follow Christ, it must be their free personal choice.

Within the Sunday Schools, teaching methods have been revolutionised by the use of visual aids, dance, drama, music making and the use of materials and lessons produced by educationalists working with, for example, Scripture Union, Scripture Press, the Christian Education Movement and the Church Pastoral Aid Society. The Church Pastoral Aid Society, among other organisations, runs courses and conferences designed to give teacher-training to those whose love of their Lord together with a love of children has led them into Sunday School work.

In the Sunday Schools there is an awareness of social

factors which may affect a child's attitude in spiritual matters. Special thought is given to children from ethnic minorities and one-parent families who come within the church setting. There is an emphasis on keeping close communication with the families. These and many other matters which have a bearing on children's religious education, spiritual development and relationship with the Church as they grow up, are covered in the material entitled *Toolbox* (previously *Noticeboard*) which the Church Pastoral Aid Society sends out to leaders of Explorer, Climber and Scrambler groups. Family services are planned to provide for a wide range of interest, intellectual ability and concentration span, so that children can look forward to coming to church along with their parents and not have to scream on Sunday mornings in order to avoid going.

Goodbye to teens

In spite of all this endeavour to provide for children in a way that fosters their spiritual growth without putting pressure on them, and makes church a place where they are welcomed and happy, the fact is that we still lose a very large number of them when they reach the age of thirteen or fourteen. Why is this?

Firstly, this is the age when children are beginning to feel their feet and emerging into adulthood. They want to question everything that they have previously taken for granted, to decide for themselves what they will think and believe and do. This is right. We want independent thinkers not zombies. We must be open to our teenagers' questions and criticisms. We must also look at our own church attendance – has it grown slack, how much is it habit, how much is it social, how much is it worship?

The foundation is laid when the children are small. They catch our enthusiasm, they find little friends in Sunday School and enjoy the varied activities and Bible stories. But this cannot last for ever and when they get to that restless stage it is better not to make an enormous issue out of going to church. It does not mean that your teenager has lost his faith. It may be simply a passing phase, and it is more likely to become a lasting antipathy if there is a battle every Sunday morning. Keep the lines of communication open and let them know that their reasoning and feelings are important to you. At the same time share your own reasons for believing that church attendance is an integral part of the Christian life. As a temporary measure it may be possible to work out some compromise. A teenager with serious questionings might undertake a course of personal Bible study. A restless soul might like to get involved with some Christian organisation or voluntary body in active outreach or charitable venture.

Be sensitive – not overbearing. This may be a formative time, when outward conformity is making way for something else. Many Christian children go through a period in their teens when they appear to be rejecting all they have been taught. This may seem very threatening to parents; but they may be feeling their way through to a first-hand faith from the second-hand faith that really belonged to their parents. They must be given the opportunity to make their personal commitment to Christ, and this is, of course, the purpose of Confirmation and believers' baptism. However, the freedom we must give them does involve the possibility of rejection. This is when we pray without ceasing.

Heavy load

When children reach this age, school pressures lay a heavy load on them. Their homework may take them the whole week-end; sports activities, music and drama rehearsals may mean late nights. Teenagers get very tired – maybe this is the time for them to switch to the evening service. In some churches where there is no formal Youth Fellowship, teenagers make the evening service a time of companionship.

148

Two-faced

Nothing can turn a teenager off church quicker than parents who attend the services regularly and just as regularly sit down at the dinner table and tear the sermon to pieces or criticise the pastor or youth leader and undermine their authority. Teenagers have a keen eye for double standards and will lose respect for an institution where the apparent pillars of the church are in fact stabbing it in the back. If there seems to be something seriously wrong with, for instance, the doctrine coming from the pulpit, it should first be quietly discussed with the man himself. We are instructed to tell the truth, but to tell it in love.

Involvement

In the junior church children have been used, for most of the time, to being gathered in small groups where they had a large measure of their leader's personal attention. When they come into the adult church they may feel to some extent distanced from what is going on. The message may lose its immediacy, and they may feel that there is little connection between their life outside and what goes on inside the church on Sundays. What can we do to encourage them to appreciate church and to look upon it as a valuable and meaningful part of their lives?

For teenagers if an activity is to have any meaning, they must feel actively involved in it. This is true also of younger children. Remember the little girl who used to scream on Sunday mornings because church was so boring? That letter continued thus: 'When I had learned to read and could join in the hymns *then* I liked it and have been faithful at church ever since.' It is participation that makes the service pleasurable, and the same principle applies from birth through childhood into the teens, though how it operates will vary:

> Jonathan has been accompanying us to church since birth. We are fortunate in that there has always been a creche where he

149

was cared for during a large part of the service or where I could escape to if he was having problems noisily! . . . He accepts church-going as naturally as taking the dog for a walk; now he is beginning to explore the hymnbook for the right number, while the churchwarden has appointed him his 'assistant' when candles are lit and hymn numbers put up. Everybody has got used to the long Sunday morning, and we relax together over our simple meal on our arrival home with a real sense of satisfaction.

Another Jonathan I know has acted as a sidesman from the age of seven, handing out the hymnbooks and welcoming the congregation. But as children grow older they tend to gravitate towards the back of the church and sit with other teenagers in a huddle on the back pews. It is as if they are getting ready to slide out of the church altogether. This is an instance of where we need to be one step ahead in our planning! In the church where I worship the Pathfinders sit in the front. They come into the first part of the service and the front two pews are reserved for them. They are now so used to sitting in an active rather than a passive part of the church that we hope it will become a habit for life and it has been a successful move as far as these youngsters are concerned, for their interest in what goes on is obvious and they do take some responsibility in the service, frequently leading the prayers or taking the collection. We are encouraged by the number staying on.

Getting and giving

Unless they are told, teenagers may not realise that God may be looking for that time in church in order to speak to them in a very personal way. Teach them to go to church expecting to receive a message from the Lord – it may not be in the sermon, it may be in a hymn, in the prayers, in someone's word of testimony, in some contact they make with a church member – they must look out for it, listen to it, take note of it and then keep it in mind during the week ahead. They must be expectant, on the alert *to get* that special word which will help them through some school crisis or be relevant to their situation in some other way. They also go to church *to give*. First to give to God the love and adoration and worship that is due; then to give to him the particular concern or burden that is on their heart, and finally to give to someone else who needs it, their smile, their encouragement and maybe their practical help. Sunday lunch can then become an exciting time of exchanging news of what God had prepared for each member of the family, a sort of de-briefing session.

Teaching

It will not make children happy in church if the teaching they receive there is different from the teaching they receive at home. It makes for the same sort of conflict as arises when a child from a Christian home is taught about evolution by an atheist. Finding the right church is so important that it should be one of the top priorities in choosing where to live and may well justify moving house.

A father who had had to move house many times in the course of his work was asked how it was that his teenagers had remained constant in their church attendance. 'We've been Methodists, Presbyterians, Episcopalians, Baptists, Assembly of God,' he replied. 'We've always felt that the key to helping our mobile family was to choose the church first, then the house.' Again:

I think that parents with families need church leaders like the ones Paul talks of in 1 Timothy 3. I feel that the leaders in most of our churches are failing us in the example they set by their liberal lifestyles, and the result of this is liberal theology coming from the pulpit. Our teenage sons go with us to church. I try to take them to where a faithful preacher is coming in to preach biblical truths . . . I would encourage other parents to stand fast, and to speak against liberal theology in the churches. We can and should trust our Lord with our children. There are many who would lead them astray, but they can, with us, be more than conquerors through him who loved us and gave himself for us.

The personal viewpoint and powerful feeling of this letter highlights the necessity for finding a church where parents feel that they can worship as a family without fear of their youngsters being pressured into a theological position that is different from their own.

Friends

Since their peers play a critical role in the lives of teenagers it is also important to find a church where there are young people of the same age as your own children. Teenagers are not very likely to stay long in a church where they look around and see only the older generation in the pews. It may be rather hurtful when children leave the church where we have brought them up in order to go to the one where their friend goes, but it is far better that they do so than stop going altogether.

Peer pressure from their non-Christian school friends may be another reason why they stop coming to church. They may be laughed at and urged to join in other activities instead. We make their lives less complicated if we help them to find an environment where their peers are Christians. One father said, 'Every time we moved to a new town the first thing we did was to look for a church with a programme for kids the ages of ours.'

Our Pathfinders come to church in the morning, then they join up with a flourishing Crusader class in the afternoon. For some who are out on a limb as Christians in the secular environment of school, this must provide a reassuring feeling of solidarity.

Puzzled by faith

There are other considerations which may give rise to a feeling of resentment against the Church. There are, for instance, problems for children when one or both of their parents are converted suddenly. Previously they were allowed to lie blissfully in bed on Sunday, listening to their radio or favourite pop cassettes until mid-day. Now dad is standing at the foot of the stairs bellowing to them to hurry up and dress and come to church. Moreover dad has stopped swearing and mum has given up smoking. They are no longer allowed to do certain things, standards are higher and discipline firmer. Certain programmes on the TV that they used to watch are now forbidden. It is a puzzling and traumatic experience when 'standards' and values in the home change suddenly and the children don't really know why. It may be very difficult, even embarrassing for a parent to try to explain the revolutionary change that has come about in his life. Nonetheless this is a time when there must be sensitivity to the feelings of children and when honest and open communication must be maintained. They must be kept in the picture, and consideration given to making the changes as smoothly as possible, and to helping the teenager through this transition period by being tactful and kindly and by being ready to admit mistakes. A teenager may be surprised by this new spirit of humility, but he will not resent it. The vulnerable parent is more likely to keep a good relationship than the authoritarian one.

The home has now virtually become a new place and everything must be committed to the Lord in trust and expectancy. A time should be set aside for studying the Bible together. This means that all members of the family have the same start, the same opportunity to ask questions, to share ideas, to learn about each other as they learn about the Lord. There is of course no guarantee that the children will also become Christians, but with prayer, with love and honesty the miracle may happen of a whole family newly united in Christ.

Resentment

Christian homes have their problems and some of these may arise from the relationship between the home and the church. It is possible for this to become a matter of resentment on the part of the children if the church claims so much of their parents' time that it appears as a threat or a rival.

Pressures on parents rub off on the children, and the more committed we are in our desire to serve the Lord, the more difficult are the decisions going to be in balancing our church work, house groups, meetings and so on, with the demands of a growing family. One seven-year-old, whose father's work kept him away from home for long hours, said 'Daddy might as well be dead.' We should be wary of giving our children the impression that they come rather low on our list of priorities and of building in them a resentment of our relationship with God. A realistic consideration of what will be involved must take place before accepting, for instance, leadership of a regular mid-week meeting. While a missed bedtime story and hurried prayers do not matter if they only happen occasionally, the time we spend with one wakeful child for whose troubled mind or body a parent is the *only* answer, may ultimately have more significance in the kingdom than a whole evening spent with a group of adults who are perfectly capable of managing on their own. Who can tell what that child may become? We are simply a small part of a meeting, but we are the only parents our children have. And why are we so afraid of being thought 'unspiritual' if we leave a meeting before the ending, when we have some anxiety about what is going on at home? Our children have been entrusted to us by God and he expects us to take care of them and train them up in the way that they should go. In later years can we complain to the late-returning teenager who has memories of waking up and calling for us in vain?

Once children arrive we have to ask ourselves if we are really indispensable in any previous commitment, though with careful planning it may be possible to adjust the domestic schedule so that everyone benefits.

When I was asked to direct a small new church choir it was with some trepidation that we began to take our child along to church every Sunday morning a full hour before service even began! With the inevitable 'teething troubles' of a new choir the problems sometimes seemed insurmountable and we would often get home exhausted and wearily steer a tired toddler through a light lunch and wonder if it was all worth it. However, even in the early days the rewards were obvious and we often reminded ourselves that the family came first and if necessary the choir would have to take second place. Now at last with Jonathan at four and a half things have become a lot easier.

Spare a thought for the pastor's kids

The children who are most likely to come under pressure through parental church commitment, are of course, the children of the pastor himself. He is in a different position from the rest of the church in that he cannot leave meetings until the last person has left. Furthermore in a busy parish it is sometimes impossible for him to take the statutory day of rest during the week. Clergy children may see very little of fathers who are at the disposal of everyone else.

Lay people must not be too demanding on overpressed clergy – they must allow their family relationships to develop, or they will not receive appropriate advice. A Canon of the church pointed out to me that people usually feel that they can speak more freely about their family problems with someone who is a family man himself. If that is so, they must see that their pastor does have time to spend with his own wife and children, for that is where the experience will come from on which he will draw to help others. Donald Carson has written:

My father was out most evenings; we saw far too little of him, and my mother bore too much of the burden. The family quiet time was not always brilliant or scintillating; indeed during particularly stressful periods of our lives it could disappear for days at a time.

However, more influential were those things that his parents 'did right'. One of these was the passing on of the biblical tradition,

> . . . without cramming it down our throats. My earliest memory is sitting in the bathtub; and when it was my father's turn to clean me up, I invariably heard a Bible story. These were *fun* times – have you ever heard the story of Naaman while you were sitting in the bath-tub? (*Evangel*).

The reduction in the number of men going into the Church has brought heavy pressure on clergy families. Many pastors have to look after several churches in country districts or enormous parishes in urban ones. The inner cities bring their own gigantic problems. The pressure which results from anxiety, lack of sleep, shortage of time for the family and financial difficulties, has made its impact on clergy life, bringing heartache and marriage break-up here as elsewhere. The fact that their parents made all major decisions jointly and maintained a united front was a stabilising factor in the lives of the Carson children:

> 'It was very difficult to get them to contradict each other, even though we children often did our best to drive a wedge between them, as children do, in the hope we could get our own way . . . They pulled together in family discipline, avoided favouritism, and thereby made the home a secure and consistent shelter . . . We grew up seeing Christianity at work. My parents weren't perfect; but more important, they weren't hypocrites. They did not simply talk about the Lord, they put their faith to work . . .`they could not and doubtless would not shield us from the drunks who occasionally came to our table, from the difficult family situations with which they sometimes had to deal . . . One of my most powerful memories concerns a Sunday morning when Dad had preached an evangelistic sermon in the church. After that

service a curious little son crept up to the study door looking for his Daddy, only to discover him weeping and praying for some of the people to whom he had just preached. If in later years I had to learn to struggle with large questions of doubt and faith, truth and revelation, obedience and world view, at least I was never burdened with a heritage of parental hypocrisy. My parents' faith was genuine and self-consistent; and there are few factors more important in the rearing and nurturing of children in a Christian home than this one (*Evangel*).

Lifeline

It is largely through the work of the churches in all their varied aspects that the children of Christian homes will be built up in the faith and enabled to resist the very heavy pressures of the secular world that awaits them.

If we think of the Church in the widest sense we must include not only all denominations but also all those other organisations that seek to put before children the simple truths of Christian belief and teach them to hold fast to those truths with courage. Among these the work of Scripture Union and of Christian Unions in schools and colleges must be recognised as playing a major role and of offering a lifeline to those children who feel isolated in their minority position as committed Christians.

Denise Trotter, one-time Scripture Union schools worker now teaching in a church primary school, has been leading a Scripture Union group in her school, and has seen it grow in numbers and enthusiasm and attract children who do not attend church or Sunday School. She herself committed her life to Christ at the age of fourteen through the witness of two Christian teachers. 'I found it very difficult to live as a Christian at school,' she recalled. 'Teenagers can be so cruel! And I found great support in the school Christian Union' (ACT).

Sue Mills works for Inter-School Christian Fellowship in secondary schools in Inner London. She described her work so:

I get involved in quite a lot of RE lessons and find that young people have no real understanding of what it means to be a Christian. They think Christianity is boring, church is boring and Christians are just people who believe in God and like 'religion'. They don't see that being a Christian actually means being involved with the Lord Jesus Christ. Most of their ideas are picked up from parents or friends and they seem to find it difficult to have an open mind and think something through for themselves. Example:

> Boy: 'The Bible's a load of rubbish.'
> Sue: 'Have you ever read it?'
> Boy: 'No. My Dad says it's a load of rubbish.'
> Sue: 'Has your Dad ever read it?'
> Boy: 'No, don't think so.'

I also visit Christian Unions and, where they don't already exist, try to help teachers to set them up. There is a strong sense of spiritual hunger among young people, but the Church hasn't shown them that there is any reality in the Christian faith, and so many kids turn to the occult and find there a spiritual reality that can only harm them.

Trying to get young Christians together and teach them is hard if you're not drawing them into a relationship with the Lord and with each other. City life tends to give young people everything on a plate with a minimum of effort on their part, and so they find it difficult to run groups because they have a lot of pressure on them and have very little time to plan and enjoy a Christian Union. My job involves helping teachers to plan programmes and take some meetings for them. I'm particularly concerned about discipling because often teenagers know that they believe in God but don't know why, and don't know how to get to know him better. When I visit churches I find that they don't understand what it's like for pupils and teachers in schools and so aren't able to support them in the ways they need.

Martial spirit

There are also those Christian organisations such as the Crusader movement, the Campaigners and the Covenanters whose martial names give a true indication of the dauntless spirit which they engender in those boys and girls who enlist under their banner through the impressionable teen years. Their influence is worldwide and the kingdom of heaven has been vastly extended because of the missionary outlook and spiritual calibre their training engenders. This combines sports, games, activities and varied interests with very thorough Bible teaching, the practice of prayer and guidelines for practical Christian living. Their hymns and choruses employ imagery which is suited to the age of youthful idealism with its need for active involvement. It cannot be denied that Christian children are involved in a ferocious battle – a battle with temptation and weakness, a battle with the secular spirit of the age treading down their faith, and a battle with the devil assaulting them through occult channels. Stirring words feed their powers of resistance. Campaigners, Covenanters and Crusaders are fired and furnished for a head on conflict with the world, the flesh and the devil. Their brief is to get up and go – wherever Christ leads them.

Of such is the kingdom

During recent years much thought has been given to children's evangelism and to the related question of the child's spiritual status. Are children all included in the kingdom of heaven unless at some point they make a conscious decision to reject Christ, or do they like adults have to 'opt in' when they reach an age of accountability; must they have a conversion experience? In his *All About Children*, John Inchley asks, 'Do I believe that no children, or only some, really belong to God until they have said "Yes" to Jesus Christ, or can I happily believe that all children belong to God until such time as they may say "No"?' Later in the book he declares that it is his belief that 'All children are included in the great atoning sacrifice and belong to Jesus Christ until they consciously reject him.'

The importance of such a belief is not only that it would eliminate any element of pressure from evangelistic methods, but that it also can allay the terrible anxiety that might otherwise assail some parents of terminally ill children, relieving them of feeling under compulsion to elicit some form of commitment from a dying child. Parents of mentally handicapped children may also receive a joyful reassurance in the belief that their child, denied a full life of the mind, is still able to participate in the full life of Christ. And there may be other Christian parents whose fear of losing a child suddenly, through accident or illness, may lead them to put a gentle sort of pressure, maybe not consciously, on their son or daughter, to 'make a decision for Christ.' In any event, undue pressure and unwise emotion should always be avoided where a child's emergent faith is concerned.

John Inchley argues his position from Scripture and also from his observation of children. He quotes the experience of a friend who said, 'I had always loved Jesus for as long as I could remember, just as I had loved my parents', and the testimony of the great preacher Campbell Morgan: 'My mother and father gave me to Christ. They never doubted the acceptance by him of their child. From infancy and through youth they trained me as his. With the result that when the time came for my personal choosing, so did I recognise the claims of his love, that without revulsion and hardly knowing when, I yielded to him my allegiance and my love.'

My own experience of children has led me to the same belief as John Inchley's. My own grandsons have both spoken quite simply and naturally, under the age of six, of belonging to Jesus. In another Christian family I know, the four children have all given their love to the Lord. Christopher, aged six, was asked what he thought about

Jesus. He replied, 'He's in heaven. He loves everybody, he cares for everybody, he made everybody. Sometimes he gives me a feeling that he's there and that he loves me. That makes me very happy.' Asked what had happened last summer, he answered, 'I gave my life to the Lord. That makes me very happy and I know that he cares for me.' Thirteen year old Nicola said that God had always been real to her. These are a few chosen from many.

Inchley also argues that there is a special sense of belonging for the children of Christian parents: 'The new life is often planted in the hearts of children of Christian parents at a very early age', and that they will turn to him is likely to be the normal experience of children of believing parents who 'give their children to Christ and, never doubting their acceptance by him, do train them as his.'

But salvation is not hereditary. Sooner or later every individual must make his or her own response to Christ. Along with all children, whatever their spiritual background, the children of Christian parents need to be given the opportunity of making their own free decision. This must entail the possibility that some will say 'No'. For them there must be no condemnation by their parents. The door of their home must ever stand open to them, with hearts full of love and welcome. We must learn from the prodigal son's father. When his son wanted to leave he didn't lock him in his room. He let him go – and he watched for his return.

Nurturing

The Reverend Clive Grinham, of the Church Pastoral Aid Society's children's department, told me how he sees the role of parents, clergy, teachers, leaders engaged in the spiritual oversight of children:

Sunday School teachers, youth leaders in church-based groups, and all who take responsibility for the spiritual

161

nurturing of children must have sensitivity to the fact that they are dealing with an impressionable age, and one at which children are very highly motivated with a desire to please. We are talking about impressing the impressionable – the child will respond to his vicar, teacher, leader in the way he thinks that person wishes him to respond and we must be wise to the fact that what is happening may not be a deep spiritual work in the heart, but the natural warm eagerness of the child to do what he feels will please the person he loves and admires. On the other hand it is pointless to be so diffident about that possibility that we miss a genuine seeking after knowledge of God in Jesus Christ or fail to see that a child is looking for support to counter the mockings from school friends who tease him or from a non-Christian home. We do not want to quench the work of the Holy Spirit in the lives of children and must remember that the children we teach will already be under pressure from all the secular influences that surround them. They need our encouragement and our firm belief. They need to be told the truth with conviction, for there will be plenty of pressures designed to undermine their emergent faith. The leader must not be 'scalp-hunting', but committing the work week by week to the Holy Spirit and seeking steady growth and a deep work of the Spirit in the children's hearts. Indeed a leader who really loves the children in his care and who also has a strong Christian faith, needs no gimmicks – needs to do no more than give simple explanations and guidelines, for faith is not taught, it is *caught*, and children will look to their leader as a model for their own commitment.

🝢 12 🝢

Moulding from Within

Let God remould your minds from within.
St Paul

In his letter to Timothy, the boy he took under his wing, Paul gives a graphic picture of what life holds in store:

> You may as well know this too, Timothy, that in the last days it is going to be very difficult to be a Christian. For people will love only themselves and their money; they will be proud and boastful, sneering at God, disobedient to their parents, ungrateful to them and thoroughly bad . . . They will think of nothing but immorality. They will be rough and cruel, sneering at those who try to be good (2 Timothy 3.3).

This all seems very familiar, and it is good to know that Timothy, apparently raised in a one-parent family, can be our classic pattern of the boy who wins through.

But this century has produced pressures that are different from ever before: the knowledge explosion and media blitz; the drug scene; 'safe sex' for kids; fear of ecological or nuclear disaster . . . In this century two discoveries have been made, both of which have the power to shape the future of the human race. One of them, nuclear power, overshadows our lives; the implications of the other, the contraceptive pill, have hardly sunk in.

Our children live under the many-faced threat of social disintegration, of universal collapse through ecological exhaustion, or of total annihilation by the bomb. One eleven-year-old said, 'There isn't much point in planning for the future because we shall all be frizzled.'

The Pill has allowed people to behave in a way they may always have wanted but would never have dared;

and one sort of permissiveness invites others, for instance a lack of regard for the rights and properties of others, drug and alcohol abuse and deviant sexual practices. Once moral absolutes, the God-given guidelines for human activity are abandoned, the way is wide open for all other evils to follow. Pornography, rape and violence escalate.

Lost allies

The allies of youth have reneged. Homes are no longer castles, nor parents pillars of strength; teachers have turned from the ancient founts of wisdom and the class-room promotes promiscuity; the Church itself is betrayed by alien voices, knowledgeable about religion but devoid of faith. Yet it is to these lost allies that the young must look for their future and their hope. They are by tradition the mentors of the young.

H. G. Wells saw human history as 'a race between education and catastrophe', and he is one among many who have seen schooling as the saviour of the human race. We know that it is not. In spite of the heroic efforts of many in the teaching profession, the same basic human failings continue to produce the same social problems and evils. Human nature does not change except by encounter with Christ and a system of education that took this into account has never been tried. If we are to look to education for answers to our problems there will have to be changes, bringing Christian belief into the content of syllabuses and its values into the hidden curriculum. The universe would then be seen as God's creation and each child as his concern. Competition would then look different; each child's unique qualities would then be acknowledged as God's gift to the future. Moral issues would replace our obsession with 'getting to the top' and fears of joblessness would go, for the purpose of work would be 'to glorify God and enjoy him forever'.

Just as children are taught about the natural laws of cause and effect, so they should be about spiritual laws, and that what you sow you do reap, even though it takes a long time. Many children are never told that there is a distinction between crime and sin; that, apart from offending against society it is possible to offend against God, and that it is right then to feel guilt. The automatic reaction is to blame someone else – usually it is 'the fault of society'.

An ISCF staff member, Tricia Williams, has observed in *ACT NOW:* 'CU members in one city tell me that one of the biggest problems for their non-Christian friends is guilt – for sins they're not sure that they've committed, because no one will admit to them when sin is sin.'

Teachers may be the only responsible adults some children meet during the course of their childhood. It is because their influence is so important that we should scrutinise the principles on which they are trained and re-align them with the spiritual dimension.

Looking to the Church

Many parents are anxious about state education, but do not wish to withdraw their children from it. Writing in the *Church of England Newspaper*, Geoff Locke has put forward the idea that the Church should supplement state education by providing Saturday morning community schools where children could be taught academic subjects from a point of view that acknowledged God as creator and man's accountability to him. This would complement the teaching of Sunday School and CYFA groups.

The Church has a formidable task in trying to salvage the young of a society that is falling apart at the seams, but the Church is not a human organisation alone. It is indwelt by the Holy Spirit, and where we see the Spirit at work, there we see society being regenerated. What is needed is the voice of faith at the top, speaking out through the media. Our laws, language, literature, proverbial sayings and culture owe so much to the Bible that Christian ideas are deep in national ways of thinking. There are millions of people longing for a safe and stable

165

future for their kids, who would associate themselves with a strong lead from the Church.

Corporate strength

Church and family must be partners. The Church encourages family life with family services, picnics, outings that all may enjoy together, and with training films such as James Dobson's *Focus on the Family*, or ones about current concerns, such as Joyce Huggett's *The Prodigal*. The concept of the church family also draws in singles and one-parent families so that all may enjoy support in their problems.

The Rev. Gordon Jessup, a team vicar in the Brammerton Group of Churches, has commented on the relationship between church, parents and children:

> In this very rural area, the Pathfinder group flourishes partly because parents are willing to turn out and transport children from up to eight tiny villages to a central point. With this impetus, the group generates a corporate strength which in turn is a magnet to keep the children coming regularly. Thus, by the grace of God, do sociological factors aid the progress of the Gospel.

Well filled

However, Scripture does not place the responsibility for bringing up children in the hands of religious institutions or schools. It places it firmly in the hands of parents. It is to parents that the words 'Train up a child in the way he should go' are addressed.

An empty tin will buckle and collapse under the pressure of deep water. A tin that is well filled will resist that pressure. It's what they have within that makes children able to resist the world's pressures. It is up to us to make that 'something within' by building the self-esteem and confidence that come from being valued in a happy home, together with the faith and courage to stand up for their beliefs.

Consider Daniel. As a teenager (at sixteen) he was seized from his home and put under formidable pressure to turn his back on it and all that it stood for. Did he buckle and collapse? No. He stuck determinedly to the codes and beliefs that had shaped his childhood, refusing the rich court food and eating his parents' simple diet, and he never ceased to affirm his faith in God by keeping up his prayers. His 'but if not . . .' is one of the most heroic assertions in the whole of history. We must bring up Daniels.

Safe base

Home must be the place where a child feels safe from whatever the world may throw at him, sure of his parents' backing, come what may. Even when he has done wrong, he knows they still love him.

He looks up to his Dad as head of the house and protector of all within, and he builds his first ideas of God on the qualities he finds in him. As Christ is head of the Church, loves her and gave himself for her, so is self-giving the father's role; that is why he is the head. A strong father holds the pressure off his children.

James Dobson has a powerful message for fathers. They have, he maintains, the power to save the family. It is their number one job to evangelise the children. 'Relay races are won or lost in the transfer of the baton, and it is here, between the generations that the baton may be dropped.'

The solidity of the home is the father's gift: the sweetness is the mother's. Scripture ascribes to God the mother's qualities as well as the father's. In our troubles God comforts us as 'one whom his mother comforteth,' and he gathers us to him 'as a hen gathers her chicks'. We undervalue the traditional home-making role of women. Making a haven for pressured children calls for intelligence and courage, limitless imagination, boundless love, unique creativity and an outpouring of energy.

Time is the enemy of the home. Many parents are over-committed and live in a state of 'routine panic' – but it takes time to get to know our children, to make the memories that they will find precious when they look back on their childhood. Memories of their closest and happiest moments – bedtime talks, country walks, shared laughter, games. It is in those moments when we transmit to them ourselves, our values, that our God becomes their God.

Self image

Self esteem is a shield against social pressure. How do we nurture it? Primarily it means a clear picture of who you are and where you have come from. 'We are these people. This is what we stand for.' Children should be acquainted with their roots, their cultural origins, national and family history. Tell them about the people and events in their past of which they may be rightly proud. See that they read the classics and learn about your writers, musicians and artists.

Cherish a sense of belonging by tracing back your family, if only for a few generations. Old photographs and letters recreate the lives and personalities of our forbears. Pass on the family jokes. Revisit meaningful places and the graves that bear your name. Commit to your children those things which you believe to be important in life – your convictions and ideas of right and wrong. Children need us to affirm our values time and again, so that they are sure of themselves outside the walls of home. And visitors too must accept their behavioural codes, mutual respect, reasonable manners. It is your child's home.

Prepare them to be different. The prestige of money, for instance, comes hard on the children of the unemployed or of Christian parents living on a low income, maybe by faith, so they must be given a different yardstick by which to see their place in the world. Be a family that appreciates good experiences above 'things' – the happiest times may cost the least.

Whenever moral choices have to be made, clarify the

issues – these are the real 'tests of life' – and emphasise that it is better to do right and fail than to achieve success by acting dishonourably. Yes, they may be teased – but children who can control their feelings are not at the mercy of teasing. They learn to control their bowels and their bodies; they can control their tempers too.

Christians are different. They are meant to be.

Help them to accept their defects. The adolescent's hypersensitivity makes him very vulnerable. He has a great need to be good-looking, brainy, rich and popular. And he may not be. But a few months make a lot of difference at this age. Help him to get things in proportion and to accept those things we cannot change. God made us and loves us just as we are. He has his purposes, and he will do what is best for us:

> I tried for Atlantic College in Wales. I wrote my essay and sent in my application. I very much wanted to go there, but I wasn't accepted. However, I have learnt so much through failing, even though it hurt at the time. I've learnt to say to God, 'I know my will took over from what you wanted me to do. The reason why I failed is because I did things my way . . . I've learnt to try, even if it looks as though I'm going to fail, and to accept the result (*Polestar*).

Nurture their strengths. Help your child to find the thing he is good at. He must be given every opportunity to develop it to the limits of his skill. Recognise every good character trait and acknowledge every victory with praise: 'That took courage – well done!' 'How very kind of you!' 'That was a sensible decision!' 'You're getting much better at keeping time/keeping your room tidy/keeping your temper.'

Be proud of them and let them know it.

Faith

Faith is the antidote to fear; courage is one of its by-products, and courage they will need. A mother wrote to me, 'Our children will have to be much better equipped for life than we ourselves were, the more so if they are to live and witness as Christian people, as God would wish them to.'

We can play our part in bringing up a generation of children whose faith can overcome fear. All sorts of domestic situations call for a sort of courage, and the way we meet setbacks and misfortunes, even maybe suffering, may be turned into learning situations that will imprint faith on our children. It grows over the years by a series of such experiences of trust.

When we talk about such issues in the light of what the Bible has to say, they learn to take it seriously as a guide to living; and in case there comes a time when they do not have their Bible, they need to learn by heart as much as possible, especially phrases for crisis situations which link faith and courage with God's promises. I was evacuated during the last war. Heartsick and lonely I started to unpack my case in the unfamiliar attic bedroom. The first thing that met my eye was a card which mother had placed on top of my clothes. 'Be strong and of good courage; fear not, neither be afraid, for the Lord thy God, he it is that doth go with thee.'

The Bible is full of ordinary people facing danger, such as Gideon, Joshua and Daniel, from which children can get a glimpse of what faith means, and the earlier the better:

> I am at last able to do some concentrated bible study by going to Fellowship classes, where my little boy, Jonathan, was enrolled in the two-year-old class. Even the little ones were taught to love the Bible, something I would not have thought possible until the age of, say, five. What a pleasure it was to help my little one to learn his first Bible verses at the age of not quite four. The joy he got from this was enormous.

There is, it seems, a germ of faith in everyone, that makes them cry out to 'someone out there' when they are in need. But prayer is more than that: it is through the daily sharing with God of all the concerns on the heart, that faith becomes a reality by which children find that they can face the playground bully, exam worries and peer pressures. They learn that what is not evident to the senses really does exist.

The pressure of change

We live in a changing world. Society is changing, children are changing, parents are changing too. They wonder what their children's growing up may mean. Soon the house will be a different place, empty of noise and laughter. What will life hold for them then? Change brings many anxieties and pressures. It can be a frightening time for all. But it is also a time of unparalleled opportunity. Girls have the same freedom as boys. Minority groups all exercise their right to have their say. Christians may be just as vocal and influential if they will only make their voices heard. It can be a challenging and a stretching time. We need to face it alongside the children. By accepting the idea of change in ourselves we will be better placed to help our children cope with the pressures of change in their lives, and to handle them with more sensitivity.

Above, and yet involved in this changing world, is the one who does not change. God does not change. He knows what is in the make-up of each child. He planned the blueprint of their genes, set them in this place at this time, and knows what the future holds for them. 'I know the plans I have for you, plans for good and not for evil, to give you a future and a hope.'

Further Reading

Adelsperger, Charlotte, *When your Child Hurts*. Augsburg 1985.

Barlow, Geoffrey, and Hill, Alison, eds, *Video Violence and Children*. Hodder & Stoughton 1985.

Batchelor, Mary, *Bringing Up a Family 0–9*. Lion 1983.

— *Bringing Up a Family 10–18*. Lion 1983.

Briscoe, Jill, *Fight for the Family*. Zondervan 1981.

Dobson, James, *Dare to Discipline*. Kingsway 1971.

— *Preparing for Adolescence*. Kingsway 1982.

— *Love Must be Tough*. Kingsway 1984.

Elliott, Michele, *Preventing Child Sexual Assault*. Bedford Square Press 1985.

Hayward, Alan, *Does God Exist? Science Says Yes*. Lakeland 1983.

Hopkinson, Anne, *Families without Fathers*. Mothers' Union 1973.

Kempe, Ruth, and Kempe, Henry, *Child Abuse*. Fontana/Open Books 1978.

Kessler, Jay, ed., *Parents and Teenagers*. Victor Books 1984.

Lawson, Michael, and Skipp, David, *Sex and That*. Lion 1985.

Leslie, Shirley, *Children Growing Up*. Scripture Union 1982.

Macaulay, Susan, *For the Children's Sake*. Kingsway 1986.

Manning, Mary, *The Drugs Menace*. Columbus Books 1985.

Porter, David, *Children at Risk*. Kingsway 1986.

Richardson, Jean, *A Death in the Family*. Lion 1979.

Sullivan, Barbara, *Your Place in the Family*. Kingsway 1983.

Townsend, Anne, *Dear Diary: My Daughter's Pregnant*. Kingsway 1984.

Townsend, Anne, and Wiltshire, Michael, *Single-handed*. Kingsway 1985.

Townsend, Anne, *Time for Change*. Marshall, Morgan & Scott 1982.

Watson, Jean, *Happy Families*. Hodder & Stoughton 1983.

White, John, *Parents in Pain*. IVP 1980.

Wynnejones, Pat, *Children, Death and Bereavement*. Scripture Union 1982.

— *Pictures on the Page. Choosing, sharing and enjoying books with children*. Lion 1982.

Useful leaflets/publications

Dear Parents and *No Entry for Parents* – sexual pressures on the young and parental rights, 25p each. *But Where is Love?* – discussion paper by a medical student for the older adolescent. All available from Family and Youth Concern.

What Parents Can Do About Drugs and *What Every Parent Should Know About Drugs*. Issued free by the DHSS (Central Office of Information).

Trend – quarterly magazine containing photo-stories and true life experiences, designed especially for the young teenager, 80p annual subscription. *Hotshot* – quarterly picture paper with stories, jokes, games and so on, for the eight to eleven year old, 60p annual subscription. Both cover moral and health education in a relevant and attractive fashion. Available from Hope Publications, Hope House, 45 Great Peter Street, London SW1P 3LT.

Videos

'Let's Talk About Love' from Family and Youth Concern. Details on page 76.

'Strong Kids, Safe Kids' from the National Children's Home.

Helpful Addresses

GENERAL

Association of Christian Teachers (Advice on problems concerned with schooling.) Richard Wilkins, 27 Spring Gardens, Garston, Watford, Herts WD2 6JJ (0923–673 485).

Child Guidance (Free counselling and support service for anyone with a child of school age or under.) Local address obtainable from school, GP, local education authority or telephone book.

Christian Action Research and Education (CARE Trust) (Advice and support for families with problems.) 21a Down Street, London W1Y 7DN (01–499 5949).

Christian Parent-Teacher League (Exists to promote parent-controlled Christian education.) 13 Pinewood Road, Eaglescliffe, Stockton-on-Tees, Cleveland TS16.

Family Holiday Association 387 City Road, London EC1V.

Family and Youth Concern (Champions the family; researches into sex education and propaganda in schools.) Valerie Riches, Wicken, Milton Keynes, Bucks MK19 6BU (0908–592 34).

Family Welfare Association (Centres for families in distress.) 501/505 Kingsland Road, London E8 4AU (01–254 6251).

National Association of Young People's Counselling and Advisory Services National Youth Bureau (Will provide information about local counselling service and befriending.) 17–23 Albion Street, Leicester LE1 6GD (0533–554 775).

National Society for Prevention of Cruelty to Children (NSPCC) (Helps parents with family problems.) 1 Riding House Street, London W1P 8AA (01–580 8812), and local branches.

Organisation for Parents under Stress (Self-help group for parents.) 29 Newmarket Way, Hornchurch, Essex, RM12 6DR (04024–515 38).

The Samaritans offer a 24–hour confidential service for people who are in despair or suicidal. Local telephone books give area numbers.

Students' Nightline (Student Samaritans based in colleges, polytechnics and universities throughout UK.) 50 Laisteridge Lane, Bradford 7, West Yorks (0274–272 43).

Westminster Pastoral Foundation (Individual and group counselling.) 23 Kensington Square, London W8 5HN (01–937 6956).

ALCOHOL, DRUGS AND SOLVENT ABUSE

Al-Anon (Advice and help for relatives and friends of problem drinkers.) Family groups: 61 Great Dover Street, London SE1 4YF (01–403 0888).

Alateen (Groups for young people aged between twelve and twenty who have an alcoholic family member.) 61 Great Dover Street, London SE1 4YF (01–403 0888).

Alcoholics Anonymous (Self-help group meetings throughout UK.) See telephone directory for local number (01–352 9799).

Band of Hope campaign against alcohol and drug abuse, and provide a quarterly teenage magazine and a lively comic for children (bi-monthly); these and teaching materials are obtainable from Hope Press, 45 Great Peter Street, London SW1P 3LT (01–222 6809).

National Campaign against Solvent Abuse (NCASA) 55 Wood Street, Mitcham Junction, Surrey (01–640 2946), and Oasis Centre, Colliers Wood, London SW19 (01–570 7166). Also Anfield Road Fellowship, 86 Anfield Road, Liverpool (051–263 3333).

Release (Counselling for people dependent on drugs,) 1 Elgin Avenue, London W9 (24–hour answering service: 01–603 8654; office hours: 01–289 1123).

The Salvation Army 110/112 Middlesex Street, London E1 7HZ (01–247 6831). Drugs Information and Advisory Service Ltd (counselling service) 111 Cowbridge Road East, Cardiff CF1 9AG (24–hour answering service: 0222–261 13).

Standing Conference on Drug Abuse (SCODA) (Information on where to find personal advice.) 3 Blackburn Road, London NW6 1XA (01–328 6556).

CHILD ABUSE

Child Assault Prevention Programme Michele Elliott, 30 Windsor Court, Moscow Road, London WC2.

Family Network, National Children's Home (Help with violence in the home, battered wives, battered children etc.) 85 Highbury Park, London N5 (01–226 2033). National Children's Home centres in major cities, day care for children. Hotline for children: 061–236 9873.

Incest Crisis Line (Confidential advice and help.) London: 01–422 5100/890 4732; Essex: 0702–584 702; Cumbria: 0965–314 32.

NSPCC National Advisory Centre on the Battered Child Denver House, The Drive, Bounds Green, London N11 (01–361 1181).

Parents Anonymous (Sympathetic advice and help for parents who feel they may abuse their children. You may remain anonymous if you wish.) 9 Manor Gardens, Islington, London N7 (24–hour answering service: 01–263 8918; office: 01–263 5672).

Rape Crisis Centre PO Box 69, London WC1 (24 hours: 01–837 1600; office: 01–278 3956).

DEATH AND BEREAVEMENT

British Guild for Sudden Infant Death Study (Sympathy and information for newly bereaved parents.) 28 Ty Gwyn Crescent, Penylan, Cardiff (0222–352 52).

The Compassionate Friends (Bereaved parents help newly bereaved parents.) National Secretary: Mrs Brenda Trimmer, 2 Norden Road, Blandford, Dorset, DT11 7LT (0258–527 60).

CRUSE (National Organisation for the Widowed and their Children) (Counselling, social contact, advice.) 126 Sheen Road, Richmond, Surrey TW9 1UR (01–940 4818).

The Foundation for the Study of Infant Deaths (Support for families bereaved by 'cot death'.) 4 Grosvenor Place, 5th Floor, London SW1X 7HD (01–235 1731/245 9421).

Stillbirth and Perinatal Death Association (Run by bereaved parents for mutual support and comfort.) 37 Christchurch Hill, London NW3 1JY (01–794 4601).

ONE-PARENT FAMILIES

Christian Link Association of Single Parents (CLASP), Linden, Shorter Avenue, Shenfield, Near Brentwood, Essex CM15 8RE (0277–221 784).

The National Council for One-Parent Families (Confidential advice and counselling, social and legal problems, housing, taxation, etc.) 255 Kentish Town Road, London NW5 2LX (01–267 1361). Also, South London Advice Centre, 20 Clapham Common South Side, London SW4 7AB (01–720 9191).

Splash (Formerly Gingerbread) (Self-help groups for single parents. Playschool and holiday schemes, crisis support, baby-sitting, advice.) 35 Wellington Road, London WC2 (01–240 0953).

SPECIAL PROBLEMS

Contact a Family (Brings together families with physically or mentally handicapped children to form local self-help groups. Activities include family support schemes, holidays, social events etc.) 16 Strutton Ground, London SW1P 2HP (01–222 2695).

Fair (For parents who are worried about their children's involvement with a cult.) Contact by letter. 2 Stone Buildings, Lincoln's Inn, London WC2A 3XB.

Hyper-active Children's Support Group (Support for parents of hyper-active children. Local self-help groups, diet sheets.) 59 Meadowside, Angmering, Sussex BN16 4BW.

John Groom's Association for the Disabled 10 Gloucester Drive, Finsbury Park, N4 2LP.

Salvation Army Tracing Missing Relatives Branch 110–112 Middlesex Street, London E1 7HZ (01–247 6831).

True Freedom Trust (Christian counselling for homosexuals.) PO Box 3, Upton, Wirral, Merseyside L49 6NY.